UML 2.0
Pocket Reference

UML 2.0
Pocket Reference

Dan Pilone

Beijing · Cambridge · Farnham · Köln · Paris · Sebastopol · Taipei · Tokyo

UML 2.0 Pocket Reference
by Dan Pilone

Copyright © 2006 O'Reilly Media, Inc. All rights reserved.
Printed in the United States of America.

Published by O'Reilly Media, Inc., 1005 Gravenstein Highway North,
Sebastopol, CA 95472.

O'Reilly books may be purchased for educational, business, or sales
promotional use. Online editions are also available for most titles
(*safari.oreilly.com*). For more information, contact our corporate/
institutional sales department: (800) 998-9938 or *corporate@oreilly.com*.

Editor: Jonathan Gennick	**Indexer:** Ellen Troutman Zaig
Production Editor: Marlowe Shaeffer	**Cover Designer:** Karen Montgomery
Copyeditor: Rachel Monaghan	**Interior Designer:** David Futato
Proofreader: Loranah Dimant	**Illustrators:** Robert Romano, Jessamyn Read, and Lesley Borash

Printing History:

March 2006:   First Edition

0-596-10208-9
[C]

Contents

UML 2.0 Pocket Reference

Introduction

Welcome to the *UML 2.0 Pocket Reference*. This book is written for an audience familiar with object-oriented programming (OOP) and the Unified Modeling Language (UML). It is not intended to teach UML from the ground up. Rather, it provides a convenient reference for those times when you know there is a way to do something but are unsure of the syntax. This book has been updated and expanded to cover UML 2.0, as defined by the Object Management Group (OMG).

TIP

If you need more than just a reminder about UML syntax, please see *UML 2.0 in a Nutshell* (O'Reilly).

UML provides a common and simple graphical representation of software design and implementation. It allows developers, architects, and experienced users to discuss the inner workings of software. UML can express detailed design at the class level, show where concurrency and parallelism can increase performance or robustness, and capture how a system must be configured and installed.

There's some debate over how to refer to UML; some authors prefer "the UML," while others prefer simply "UML." Strictly speaking, "the UML" is grammatically correct; however, this book uses the more colloquial "UML."

Whenever it is helpful to clarify UML syntax or semantics, this book compares UML to a concrete language mapping in Java™ or C++.

Typographic Conventions

The following typographic conventions are used in this book:

`Constant width`

> Used in UML syntax diagrams and in text to refer to class names, stereotype names, property names, and other text taken from diagrams in this book.

`Constant width italic`

> Used in UML syntax diagrams to indicate user-supplied elements.

Italic

> Used to introduce new terms and indicate URLs and filenames.

...

> Indicates where nonessential material has been omitted for clarity in an example.

Note that UML makes frequent use of curly braces ({}) and guillemots («»). When used in a syntax definition, they are required by UML.

Acknowledgments

This book would not have been possible without the support of several people. First, I'd like to thank my editor, Jonathan Gennick, for his hard work, excellent advice, and nearly limitless patience.

Next, I'd like to thank the technical reviewers of the first edition, Donald Bales and David Thomson. Their experience and knowledge helped make this book what it is.

Finally, I'd like to thank my family for putting up with another book authoring "process"—specifically, our newest edition, Nick, who slept long enough at night to let me get this book finished—and to my wife, Tracey, who ran interference with our oldest son enough for most of this book's content to be coherent.

UML 2.0 Overview

First and foremost, UML is a language. There are rules governing how things can be combined to form expressions. The idea is that UML doesn't just give you a way to draw diagrams, but it gives you a way to express concepts and relationships. To support this, UML needs very specific terms for elements; however, as with any language in common use, these terms are muddied in practice. For example, an *operation* in UML is an abstract concept defining an action on an interface, while a *method* is a concrete implementation. In the real world, these two terms are often used interchangeably. Throughout this book, I will use the UML-specific term to avoid confusion.

UML is documented in four specifications from the OMG (*http://www.omg.org*):

- The Diagram Interchange
- The UML Infrastructure
- The UML Superstructure
- The Object Constraint Language

Together, these specifications account for over 1,000 pages of UML goodness. These are the definitive sources for UML; however, the OMG has explicitly designed UML to be extended and customized to whichever domain it is being applied. For most UML users, the UML Superstructure is the document of interest. It provides a detailed explanation of UML elements and will be the focus of this book.

Why UML 2.0?

UML 2.0 represents a significant update from previous versions. One of its major goals is to offer better support for automation and modeling tools. To this end, several of the core UML concepts have been formalized and documented so they can be modeled, extended, and even executed by development and design applications. This approach to software development is called Model Driven Architecture (MDA), and though it is the subject of many books, MDA will not be discussed in this one.

For the average modeler, UML 2.0 offers a much more consistent and refined notation and introduces several new diagrams. For example, UML 2.0 now supports Composite Structure Diagrams, which capture design and architectural patterns and show how they are used in an application. From the behavioral modeling side, UML 2.0 groups several types of behavior diagrams under the umbrella term of Interaction Diagrams, which includes Sequence Diagrams (with much-needed support for looping and conditionals), Activity Diagrams, Timing Diagrams, and more.

General Modeling Guidelines

There are several key concepts to keep in mind when modeling with UML:

Nearly everything in UML is optional

UML is designed to be tailored to your project or organization, so just about every element is optional. This makes UML very flexible, but it can also be confusing if it is not handled carefully. When modeling, use the parts of a diagram that help you convey your message. Using more than what's needed (or worse, trying to use every symbol supported by a diagram) only clutters a diagram. Admittedly, knowing what's needed (and what isn't) is somewhat a matter of experience and somewhat a matter of trial and error. A small development shop of 4 developers may need a lot less formality in their diagrams than a distributed team of 100 developers. I will make note of places where parts of the syntax are mandatory.

Models are rarely complete

Because so much of UML is optional, it is difficult to have a complete model. This gets somewhat easier with a good modeling tool and a very disciplined development process, but, in practice, models are used to convey only as much detail as needed. If you're intending to use your model in an MDA environment, you'll need much more detail than if you're sketching ideas on a whiteboard. Your model does not need to be complete to be effective; it just needs to be able to communicate the necessary information.

UML is open to interpretation

The UML specification defines how elements of UML relate to each other, but it does not discuss how UML maps to a particular language. What a specific notation means in the context of a diagram is often up to the organization using it. For example, some groups use composition to indicate a C++ reference and aggregation to indicate a C++ pointer. Although this is not discussed in the UML specification, there's nothing wrong with using this approach to modeling as long as you're consistent.

UML is designed to be extended

UML includes several mechanisms—stereotypes and profiles are the two most common—to specialize it for a particular domain. Developing a full profile is beyond the scope of this pocket reference, but be aware that it is available to you. There are several formal profiles available for things such as J2EE and database modeling. If you're going to be modeling a complex domain, consider putting together a profile. (By complex, I do not necessarily mean software modeling; financial and business process modeling are also prime candidates for UML profiles.)

Static Modeling with UML

Static modeling captures the fixed, code-level relationships contained within a system. Static modeling encompasses the following diagram types:

- Class diagrams
- Package diagrams
- Component diagrams
- Composite Structure diagrams
- Deployment diagrams

Static modeling, by definition, does not include dynamic specifications (e.g., concurrency), state transitions, or object lifetimes and communication (see the later sections "Activity Diagrams," "Statechart Diagrams," and "Interaction Diagrams," respectively).

UML Classifiers

Static modeling makes heavy use of UML classifiers. A *UML classifier* is a set of UML elements that has something in common, such as attributes, methods, etc. UML defines many classifiers, but the following are the most common:

Class
> A class describes a name, attributes, operations, and responsibilities that are shared by multiple objects. Classes are blueprints for runtime objects.

Component
> A component is a physical piece of a system that realizes one or more interfaces. It is similar to a subsystem, but it is typically smaller and contained within a more encompassing subsystem.

Datatype

A datatype is a fundamental type that is usually built into an implementation language. For example, C++ supports int, double, char, and so forth.

Interface

An interface provides operation signatures but no implementations. It is typically used to define a service that one or more classes implement or realize (see the subsection "Realization" in "Class relationships," later in this book).

Node

A node is a physical installation of the system at runtime. Nodes are used in deployment diagrams to show how various pieces of the system relate at a higher level than classes, components, or even subsystems. A node is typically used to represent distinct pieces of the system that may reside on one or more computers.

Signal

A signal represents an asynchronous call between two instances of a class. Signals are commonly used in modeling message-passing systems to show the various messages.

Subsystem

A subsystem is similar to a component in that it provides a realization of one or more interfaces. A subsystem is almost always made up of multiple classes, and it often contains multiple components.

Use case

A use case is a collection of requirements for a system, described as a sequence of interactions with the user. A single system has many use cases, each providing some measurable piece of functionality when invoked by the user.

Stereotypes

All static UML diagrams share several UML elements and extension mechanisms. One such mechanism is UML *stereotypes*. Stereotypes provide a way of extending UML by defining simple terms and using them to clarify UML elements and their participation in a system. Stereotypes are usually one word, such as interface, exception, import, or library. See the end of this section for a list of common stereotypes.

You can define a set of related stereotypes to model a specific area, such as J2EE or Business Marketing. You can then group these stereotypes with tagged values (see the later section "Tagged Values") into a UML *profile*. There are several UML profiles available and the OMG encourages you to create your own if your domain warrants it.

Stereotypes are displayed between « and » near or within the stereotyped element. In Figure 1, ChecksumValidator is marked as a utility class, whereas InvalidChecksumException is identified as an exception.

Figure 1. A simple class diagram showing stereotypes

Rather than show stereotypes in the textual form, UML allows you to define an icon to represent a stereotype graphically. For example, the stick-and-lollipop representation of interfaces (described later in the "Class Diagrams" section) is a graphical, iconic representation of the interface stereotype.

Stereotypes apply to nearly all of UML, though some make sense only when attached to the correct type of element. The following is a list of common predefined UML stereotypes and the UML elements to which they may apply. You can define additional stereotypes as needed.

Actor

Applies to a class. Represents a specific role related to performing a use case.

Access

Applies to a dependency. Shows that the originating package uses the public elements of the ending package.

Association

Applies to the end of a link. Shows that the ending object has an associative relationship with the object at the other end of the link.

Become

Applies to a message. Shows that the ending object is the same as the sender of the message, though it may have changed values or state.

Bind

Applies to a dependency. Shows that the originating class instantiates the ending template with the specified template parameters.

Call

Applies to a dependency. Shows that the originating operation calls the ending operation.

Copy

Applies to a message. Shows that the target element is an exact copy of the source element.

Create

Applies to an event or message. Shows that the ending element is created by the source element.

Derive

Applies to a dependency. Shows that the originating element can be derived from the ending element.

Destroy

Applies to an event or message. Shows that the ending element is destroyed as a result of the event or message.

Document

Applies to a component. Shows that the given component is a document.

Enumeration

Applies to a class. Shows that the class is an enumeration.

Exception

Applies to a class. Shows that the class is an exception.

Executable

Applies to a component. Shows that the component can be executed.

Extend

Applies to a dependency. Shows that the originating use case extends the ending use case.

Facade

Applies to a package. Shows that the stereotyped package is actually a controlled view into another package.

File

Applies to a component. Shows that the stereotyped component is a file containing code or data.

Framework

Applies to a package. Shows that the stereotyped package contains implementations of design or architectural patterns.

Friend

Applies to a dependency. Shows that the originating element is not bound by the usual visibility constraints of the ending element.

Global

Applies to the end of a link. Shows that the ending element is visible in the global scope.

Import
> Applies to a dependency. Shows that the public elements of the ending package are imported into the namespace of the originating package.

Implementation
> Applies to a generalization. Shows that the descendant class inherits its parent's implementation but does not honor the substitution principle and cannot be used as a replacement for its superclass.

ImplementationClass
> Applies to a class. Shows that the stereotyped class is an implementation in a specific programming language.

Include
> Applies to a dependency. Shows that the originating use case incorporates the behavior of the ending use case.

InstanceOf
> Applies to a dependency. Shows that the originating object is an instance of the ending class.

Instantiate
> Applies to a dependency. Shows that the originating class creates objects of the ending class.

Interface
> Applies to a class. Shows that the operations on the stereotyped class define a service that the class represents.

Invariant
> Applies to a constraint. Shows that the constraint must always be true.

Library
> Applies to a component. Shows that the stereotyped component is either a static or dynamic library.

Local
> Applies to the end of a link. Shows that the ending object is in the local scope.

Metaclass

Applies to a UML classifier. Shows that a classifier's instances (objects) are classes.

Model

Applies to a package. Shows that the package is a self-contained representation of a system.

Parameter

Applies to the end of a link. Shows that the object is a parameter.

Postcondition

Applies to a constraint. Shows that the constraint must be true after the execution of an operation.

Powertype

Applies to a class or dependency. Shows a classifier whose instances (objects) are children of the given parent.

Precondition

Applies to a constraint. Shows that the constraint must be true before executing an operation.

Process

Applies to a class. Shows a classifier whose instances are full operating-system processes.

Refine

Applies to a dependency. Shows that the originating element is a further refinement (less abstract) than the ending element.

Requirement

Applies to a comment or note. Shows that the comment or note represents a requirement of a system.

Responsibility

Applies to a comment. Shows that the comment represents a responsibility of an associated class.

Self

Applies to the end of a link. Shows that the ending object is the same object as the source message.

Send

Applies to a dependency. Shows that the originating operation sends the ending event.

Signal

Applies to a class. Shows that a class represents an asynchronous piece of information exchanged between objects.

Stereotype

Applies to a class. Shows that the class is actually a stereotype that can be applied to other elements.

Stub

Applies to a package. Shows that the stereotyped package acts as a fake (stubbed) version of another package.

Subsystem

Applies to a package. Shows that the stereotyped package contains a group of related functionality, which can be implemented with other unexposed elements.

System

Applies to a package. Shows that the stereotyped package contains a complete system.

Table

Applies to a component. Shows that the stereotyped component represents a database table.

Thread

Applies to a class. Shows that instances of the class are lightweight operating-system threads.

Trace

Applies to a dependency. Shows that the originating element is an earlier (in execution time) version of the ending element.

Type

> Applies to a class. Shows that the class represents the structure and responsibilities of an object but not its implementation. Similar to an abstract class.

Use

> Applies to a dependency. Shows that the originating element uses the ending element's public interface.

Utility

> Applies to a class. Shows that the class's attributes and operations are of classifier scope (static). Typically, such a class is not instantiated.

Notes

All diagrams support the use of UML notes. *Notes* are simply text added by the modeler to include outside information that is not captured in UML. For example, the modeler may use notes to present questions or comments to the developers, provide a URL to a detailed requirements document, or introduce a snippet of pseudocode to help explain a relationship.

Notes are represented as dog-eared rectangles, as shown in Figure 2.

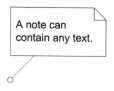

Figure 2. A UML note

Notes can be placed anywhere on a diagram and can be connected to one or more UML elements using the *note anchor line*, which is the dashed line shown in Figure 3.

This class should probably be implemented natively for performance reasons.
«utility»
ChecksumValidator

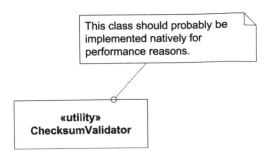

Figure 3. An anchored note

UML predefines the `requirements` stereotype for use with notes. Unsurprisingly, this stereotype is used to show that a given note contains system requirements.

Tagged Values

UML elements support the use of tagged values to specify user-defined properties for an element. These properties apply to the element itself and typically contain metadata external to the runtime information of a system, such as information used by a packager or the execution environment. Common uses for tagged values include conveying author name, version, or dependency information. Figure 4 shows author and version tags on a simple class.

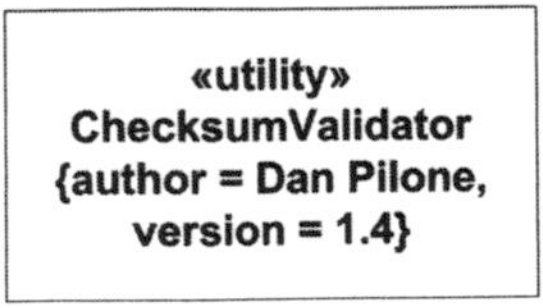

«utility»
ChecksumValidator
{author = Dan Pilone,
version = 1.4}

Figure 4. A class with tagged values

The tagged-value syntax is simply:

```
{ tag = value }
```

This syntax includes the following user-defined elements:

tag

A short textual name of the property. Technically, this is optional if the property to which the value applies is unambiguous; however, I highly recommend that you use tags to avoid any possible confusion.

value

The actual value of the property. The type and syntax of the value depends on the property.

UML predefines the following four properties, but you can add more as needed:

documentation

This property is usable on any element and contains the documentation for the element. Some tools support this property but show the information in another compartment or window or only in generated code.

location

This property applies to most elements and identifies where an element executes. The value of this property typically references a node or component defined in a system. (See "Deployment Diagrams," later in the text, for more information.)

persistence

This property applies to classes, associations, and attributes (see the upcoming section "Class Diagrams" for more information). Persistence refers to whether an element's value is saved when a system is restarted. The suggested values are persistent and transient.

semantics

This property applies to classes and operations and is similar to documentation (see "Class Diagrams," later in this book). The value of this property details the element and its intent.

Constraints

Relationships between elements, as well as the elements themselves, can be validated using constraints. *Constraints* allow you to express conditions that must be true for the model to be valid. As with tagged values, constraints are specified between braces and they are textual representations of a condition. Constraints have the following syntax:

```
{ textual constraint }
```

The textual constraint may consist of simple expressions, full sentences, or formal constraint syntax. UML defines a formal grammar named the *Object Constraint Language* (OCL). The final section of this book gives a brief summary of key OCL syntax, but it is described in more detail in *UML 2.0 in a Nutshell* (O'Reilly) and *The Unified Modeling Language Reference Manual* (Addison Wesley).

Constraints can be placed near the constrained element or linked between relationships by using a dashed line, as shown in Figure 5.

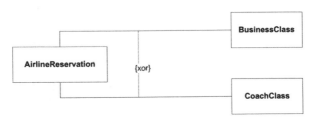

Figure 5. An example constraint

Alternatively, UML allows constraints to be placed in notes and attached to the associated element.

The following are some of the more common UML constraints, although the modeler can add more as needed:

Complete
> Applies to a generalization. Shows that the subclasses of the element are the final descendants of the superclass.

Destroyed

> Applies to an instance or end of a link. Shows that the instance or link is destroyed upon completion of the operation.

Disjoint

> Applies to a generalization. Indicates that an instance of the superclass cannot be an instance of more than one of its subclasses. This is the default reading of a generalization.

Implicit

> Applies to an association. Specifies that the relationship does not physically exist but is implied semantically.

Incomplete

> Applies to a generalization. Shows that not all the subclasses have been shown and that other subclasses are permitted.

New

> Applies to an instance or link. Shows that the instance or link is created as a result of the operation.

Overlapping

> Applies to a generalization. Indicates that an instance of the superclass can be an instance of more than one of its subclasses. However, this constraint does not guarantee that will happen; it merely allows it to happen.

Transient

> Applies to an instance or link. Shows that the instance or link is created during the execution of an operation but is destroyed before the operation completes.

Xor

> Applies to multiple associations. Shows that for the constrained associations, only one association actually exists for a given object.

Class Diagrams

Class diagrams are used to model the static relationships between components of a system. A single UML model can have many class diagrams showing the same system from different views. For example, a class diagram may show several classes using a subsystem interface but not elaborate on the details of the subsystem implementation. A different class diagram, one used by the subsystem developers, may show both the subsystem interface and the classes that help realize that subsystem.

Figure 6 shows a sample class diagram.

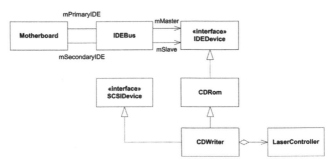

Figure 6. A sample class diagram

Classes

Classes represent concepts within a system, and they are typically named using nouns. A single class represents one or more objects in the system at runtime. (Class multiplicity is explained in more detail later in this section.)

Each class is made up of multiple compartments. Compartments can be named or anonymous. In its simplest form, a class has just one anonymous compartment showing the class's name, as shown in Figure 7.

```
┌─────────────────────────┐
│                         │
│         Student         │
│                         │
│                         │
└─────────────────────────┘
```

Figure 7. A class with only a name compartment

A more common representation consists of three compartments: one showing the class's name, one showing its attributes, and one showing its operations (see "Attributes" and "Operations" later in the book). Additional compartments can be added when needed—for example, to show responsibilities, exceptions, or mutexes. Figure 8 shows several compartments in a class.

```
┌───────────────────────────────────────────────────┐
│                ReservationController               │
├───────────────────────────────────────────────────┤
│ -departureTime : Date                              │
├───────────────────────────────────────────────────┤
│ + setDepartureTime (reservation: int, time: Date): void │
└───────────────────────────────────────────────────┘
```

Figure 8. Anonymous and named compartments

Classes can appear on multiple class diagrams and need not show all of their detail on every diagram. It is a common practice to hide (or *elide*) operations and attributes that are not relevant to a given diagram. Such omitted operations and attributes are often indicated by an ellipsis (...), as shown in Figure 9.

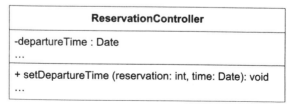

Figure 9. A sample class with elided attributes and operations

---

Class names, pathnames, and scope

Class names are usually made up of letters but can include numbers. Though a name can be arbitrarily long and include punctuation, it is uncommon to use any punctuation other than underscoring. Colons are not permitted, as they are used to divide the components of the full pathname of the class.

Pathnames are used to represent scope, as each class within the same scope must be named uniquely. For example, the following fully qualified names refer to different classes:

```
com::oreilly::editor::SpellChecker
org::openoffice::editor::SpellChecker
```

The names before SpellChecker refer to the containing packages (see "Package Diagrams" later in this book).

Multiplicity

As with other components of UML, the multiplicity of a class can be specified by placing a number in the upper-right corner of the top-most compartment, as shown in Figure 10.

Figure 10. Class multiplicity (showing a singleton)

Classes differ from typical UML multiplicity because without a multiplicity specifier, classes default to more than one allowable instance. For example, as shown earlier in Figure 6, the Motherboard class can be instantiated multiple times. However, specifying a multiplicity of 1 indicates that the class should be a singleton (as illustrated in Figure 10). It is not uncommon to see a singleton class stereotyped with <<singleton>>, but this stereotype is not officially part of UML.

Attributes

Attributes represent common features of a class. For example, a Car class would include attributes representing color, make, model, year of production, etc. Attributes can be represented using two different notations: inlined or as relationships between classes.

Inlined attributes

You show inlined attributes of a class in the second compartment, as shown in Figure 11.

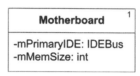

Figure 11. Example attributes

An inlined attribute is written as follows:

```
visibility / attributeName : attributeType
multiplicity = defaultValue
{properties and constraints}
```

This syntax contains the following user-defined elements:

visibility

Shown as +, #, -, or ~ for *public*, *protected*, *private*, or *package*, respectively. If no visibility specifier is used, the attribute is public by default.

/

Indicates this attribute is derived. A derived attribute can be computed from other attributes, and it may not need to actually be stored in implementation. For example, the area of a square could be computed from its length and width. If both the length and width are captured, the modeler could mark the area attribute as derived.

---

attributeType
> Indicates the type of the attribute. Usually, the attribute type is the name of another class or a basic type, such as integer or string.

multiplicity
> Indicates the multiplicity of the attribute. Typically, the attribute is represented as an array or vector, depending on the language. The multiplicity is expressed as a number, several numbers separated by commas, or a range of numbers between square brackets (e.g., [2], [3,7,9], [10.. 20]). You can use an asterisk (*) by itself to represent "0 or more" or with a number, as in [2..*] for "2 or more." If not specified, the default multiplicity is 1.

property and constraints
> Properties are tags that you can attach to attributes to provide more information. They can be context-specific, such as J2EE configuration options or concurrency controls; however, they are most commonly used to denote ordering or uniqueness. See "Properties," later in this section, for more information.
>
> Constraints are one or more restrictions placed on an attribute. See "Constraints" in "Static Modeling with UML," earlier in the text.

Static attributes

Attributes can be specific to an instance or object of a class, in which case, they are considered to be of *instance scope*. Attributes can also be shared between classes (static in C++ or Java), in which case, they are considered to be of *classifier scope*. Attributes with classifier scope are underlined in the class, as shown in Figure 12.

Figure 12. A classifier (static) attribute

Properties

UML provides several built-in properties that you can use to refine your attribute specification. Each property can be used individually or combined with other properties or constraints as needed.

UML uses a set of specific properties after an attribute's type to indicate the attribute's order and multiplicity. If the multiplicity of an attribute is greater than 1, you can specify that the attribute must be ordered. The exact meaning of "ordered" depends on the attribute, but UML states that the attributes must be stored sequentially. For numerical types, this is relatively straightforward. For more complex types, it is implementation-dependent, but imagine using alphabetical order for strings or a user-defined sorting specification for larger objects. To specify that an attribute must be ordered, place the keyword ordered in curly braces ({}) after the attribute.

In addition to being ordered, attributes with multiplicity greater than 1 can be required to be unique, meaning that there can be no duplicate values. *By default, attributes with multiplicity greater than 1 are unique!* For example, a list of student names (strings) cannot, by default, have the same name listed twice. To specify that your attribute's elements should be unique, use the property unique in curly braces ({}) after the attribute. To allow duplicates, use the property not unique. Figure 13 shows order and uniqueness on attributes.

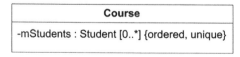

Figure 13. A class with an ordered and unique collection

UML specifies a set of mappings, from order and uniqueness specifications to collection types, that holds an attribute's values. Table 1 shows how each combination of order and uniqueness translates to a collection type. Note that the types specified here are UML types—a particular language may change this mapping or offer only a limited set of collection types.

Table 1. Collection types for ordered and uniqueness properties

Ordered	Uniqueness	Collection type
False	False	Bag
True	True	OrderedSet
False	True	Set
True	False	Sequence

In addition to order and uniqueness, UML defines several properties for use with attributes. The following are the most commonly used:

readOnly
> States that the attribute may not be modified once a value has been set. This typically maps to const in a programming language.

union
> States that the attribute type is a union of the possible values for this attribute. Usually, used with derived attributes to indicate that the attribute type is a union of the derived attributes' types.

subsets <attribute-name>
> States that the attribute's type is a subset of all of the valid values.

redefines <attribute-name>
> States that the attribute acts as an alias for the given attribute. This can be used to show that a subclass has an attribute that is an alias for a superclass's attribute.

composite
> States that the attribute is a part of a whole-part relationship with the owning class.

Class relationships

Attributes can also be represented using a class relationship notation. In this notation, a line is drawn between the owning class and the target attribute's class. The relationship notation produces a larger class diagram (because there are more classes to show), but it gives a quick visual indication of which classes are related.

To connect two classes, use one of the association relationships described in Figures 16 through 21. You can capture the same information that you can with inlined attributes, though with slightly different notation. The style of the line used to connect two classes is significant and represents the strength of the relationship. Figure 14 shows an example of a class with an attribute in relationship notation.

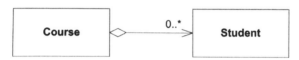

Figure 14. Aggregation between two classes

Dependency. Dependency is the weakest relationship; it indicates only a loose coupling between two classes. It is typically read as "uses a," as in "ClassA uses a ClassB." A dependency relationship is represented by a dashed line with an arrow pointing to the target class. Usually, a dependency represents a relationship in which the class on the left side of the arrow briefly uses the class on the right—for example, as a return type or parameter related to an operation. Figure 15 shows an example of a simple class dependency in which ChecksumValidator is dependent on InvalidChecksumException.

Figure 15. A class dependency

Association. An association indicates a stronger relationship between two classes than a dependency does. It is typically read as "has a," as in "ClassA has a ClassB." An association is represented by a solid line between two classes. Classes bound by associations have a persistent relationship that usually exists longer than a single method call.

Associations can indicate one- or two-way navigation, depending on the presence of an arrow showing the direction of navigability. Technically, an association line without arrows doesn't tell you anything about navigability; however, it is typically used to indicate navigability in both directions. You can explicitly forbid navigation in a particular direction by placing a small *x* (two crossed lines, not necessarily the letter *x*) near the end of the non-navigable class. Figure 16 shows variations of navigability. Notice the small *x* next to Student.

Figure 16. An association with one-way navigability

Associations can be named at either or both ends to indicate the roles that the association plays. As shown in Figure 17, the two instances of IDEBus are identified as PrimaryIDE and SecondaryIDE within one Motherboard.

You can specify attribute names by placing an attribute's visibility and name near the association line, as shown in Figure 18.

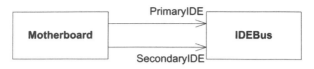

Figure 17. An association with roles

Figure 18. Naming attributes using association

Using relationship notation, you can place constraints *between* attributes. You indicate a constraint by drawing a dotted line between the association lines and writing the constraint near it. When using inline attribute notation, you need to capture constraints between attributes in a note. By using the standard UML notation for constraints, you can place a constraint directly on an association. See the earlier section "Constraints" for more information on constraint syntax. Figure 19 shows constraints between attributes.

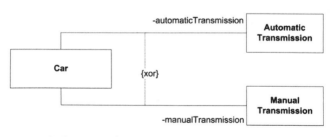

Figure 19. Constraints between attributes

Multiplicity of each class in an association can be specified at the respective end of an association line. If none is specified, a multiplicity of 1 is assumed. Multiplicity in an association is specified in the same way that any other UML multiplicity is specified: as a single number, as a range, or as comma-separated values. An asterisk (*) is used to represent any number. Figure 20 shows a multiplicity specification for an association that allows one Reservation to have one or more FlightLegs.

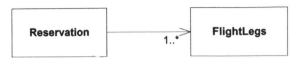

Figure 20. An association with multiplicity

Finally, associations can be named. Names are short phrases that help describe the relationship captured by an association. They are usually applicable when reading an association in a certain direction, so UML recommends placing a triangle at the appropriate end of the name to show the direction in which it should be read. The name doesn't have any technical meaning; it is used to help the reader understand your association. Figure 21 shows a named association.

Figure 21. A named association

In Figure 21, the triangle indicates that the association name should be read from left to right, as Motherboard Communicates Using IDEBus. Arrows are helpful particularly when layout constraints force you to present associations in an order contrary to the natural order for the language you are using.

Aggregation. Aggregation is a special type of association used to represent a stronger relationship between two classes than regular associations. It is usually read as "owns a," as in "ClassA owns a ClassB." An aggregation is represented as a solid line with a diamond at one end and an arrow at the other end. The containing class is on the diamond side of the line, with the arrow pointing to the class that it contains.

As with associations, aggregations can be bidirectional, though they are typically navigable only from the containing class to the contained class. Objects in an aggregation relationship do not necessarily share a lifetime, but an aggregation indicates that they are intimately related. For example, a Division of a company may contain several Employees. The employees could be transferred to other divisions, or related to customers, etc., but the Division aggregates them together. If your relationship is more of a whole-part relationship, you may be better off with a composition relationship, described in the next section.

Also, as with associations, aggregations can be refined further with constraints, tagged values, and multiplicity indicators. Figure 22 shows an aggregation between a company division and employees.

Figure 22. Aggregation relationships

Composition. Composition is the strongest relationship between two classes. It is usually read as "is made up of," as in "Class A is made up of ClassB" (or "ClassB is part of ClassA," depending on how you read it). Composition is a special form of aggregation that indicates not only lifetime association, but typically exclusive containment as well. The UML specification allows the contained object to be passed to another object to be preserved, but conceptually, it shouldn't stand on its own if the composite class is destroyed. There is debate over when composition is more appropriate than aggregation; some people argue that composition should never be used at all.

Frequently, composition is used to indicate exactly how a relationship should be represented in generated code. For example, in C++, aggregations are typically represented as pointers or references, while composition is typically represented by physically containing an instance of the aggregate class. In Java, composition is often used to show relationships with inner classes.

Composition is represented by a solid line with a filled diamond at one end and an arrow at the other end. The diamond is on the side of the larger, containing class, whereas the arrow points to the smaller, part class. As with aggregations, composition relationships can be refined with constraints, tagged values, and multiplicity indicators. Figure 23 shows class composition.

Figure 23. A composition relationship

Generalization. Generalization is used to show inheritance; subclass B has an "is a" relationship with superclass A, or superclass A is a generalization of subclass B. A single class can inherit from multiple superclasses, though language mappings might not support this. For example, C++ supports multiple inheritance, whereas Java does not. Generalization does not require the more specific class to provide operation implementations, so an interface can inherit another interface.

Generalization is represented by a solid line with a closed arrow pointing to the superclass. Generalizations are not typically named or adorned with any other information. Figure 24 shows a generalization relationship between two classes, indicating that FlightReservation inherits from Reservation.

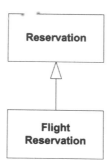

Figure 24. Class generalization

Realization. Realization indicates that a class implements, or *realizes*, an interface at the other end (see the upcoming section, "Interfaces"). Similar to inheritance, realization indicates that the class realizing an interface is an implementation of the referenced interface. While interfaces define only operation signatures, a realization ties an interface to a concrete implementation (e.g., to a concrete set of methods). It is not uncommon to show packages (stereotyped as subsystems) or components realizing interfaces. A single class can realize multiple interfaces. Because interfaces cannot have implementations, an interface cannot realize another interface.

Realization is represented by a dashed line with a closed arrow pointing to the interface. Figure 25 shows a class realizing an interface.

UML defines an alternate representation of interface realization, named the *stick-and-lollipop* notation, as shown in Figure 26.

Association classes

There are times when the relationship between two classes has information that you want to capture. For example, an insurance company assigns insurance agents to regional sales teams. The agent and the company still have a relationship,

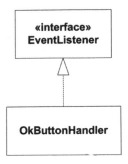

Figure 25. Interface realization

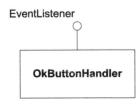

Figure 26. Stick-and-lollipop notation for interfaces

but there is an entity between them. You can use an *association class* to capture this information. An association class is represented by a dashed line from a relationship to the class capturing the additional information. Figure 27 shows an example of an association class.

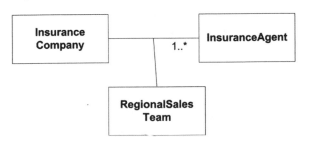

Figure 27. An association class

Association qualifiers

Often, relationships between larger entities and smaller entities are keyed by some unique value. For example, a library may identify a book by its Dewey Decimal Number. You can show this unique key relationship using an *association qualifier*. An association qualifier is represented as a smaller rectangle at the larger end of a relationship. The name of the qualifier is written in the rectangle. Figure 28 shows a library and its association to books.

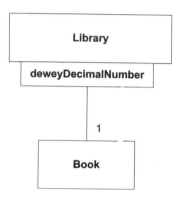

Figure 28. An association qualifier identifying a unique book

Operations

Operations indicate what a class can do, sometimes referred to as its responsibilities. Operations are typically represented in the third compartment of a class, as shown in Figure 29.

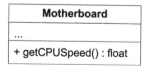

Figure 29. An example operation

As with attributes, operations can be elided (...) when they are not relevant to the current diagram. An operation is defined as follows:

```
visibility operationName
(parameterList) : returnType
{property and constraints}
```

This syntax includes the following user-defined values:

visibility

Shown as +, #, -, or ~, for *public*, *protected*, *private*, or *package,* respectively. If the visibility of an operation is not shown, the operation is public by default.

parameterList

Shows the arguments to the operation. If there is more than one parameter, simply separate parameters with a comma. The syntax for parameters is as follows:

```
(direction parameterName
: parameterType [multiplicity] = defaultValue)
{properties and constraints}
```

This syntax contains the following user-defined values:

direction

Indicates whether the parameter is an input value (unmodifiable), an output value, or both. It is optional, but if specified, it must be specified as in, out, or inout.

parameterName

A valid UML name.

parameterType

Indicates the type of the parameter. Typically, the parameter type is a class name or a basic type, such as integer or string.

multiplicity

Specifies how many instances of the parameter are required. If it's not specified, the default is a multiplicity of 1. Otherwise, you can specify a range of

values, specific integer values, or an asterisk (*) to
mean unlimited instances.

defaultValue
> The initial value of the parameter if a value is not
> specified by the caller.

returnType
> The return type of the operation. Usually, the return type
> is a class name or a basic type, such as integer or string.

constraints
> Provides additional information about an operation. See
> the upcoming section, "Properties and constraints on
> operations."

Polymorphism

UML makes a distinction between an operation and a
method. An *operation* is a signature that defines the operation name, its arguments, and its return type, whereas a
method is an implementation of an operation. Multiple
classes in an inheritance hierarchy can have the same operation. For example, they each may define an edit operation,
but each class may define its own implementation of that
operation.

Operations are polymorphic by default, meaning that subclasses (classes further down the inheritance hierarchy) can
provide their own implementation of an operation rather
than inherit their parent's method. However, the leaf property is used to state that the given operation cannot be overridden by subclasses. The leaf property is mapped to final
in Java and non-virtual in C++.

Abstract operations

Unlike attributes, operations can be abstract, meaning the
class provides no implementation. Italics indicate abstract-
operation names.

A class that does not have an implementation for an operation (method), either through inheritance or by providing one itself, is considered an *abstract class* and its name is italicized. You cannot create an instance of an abstract class; however, they can be subclassed to provide implementation details. A purely abstract class (one with no methods at all) is similar to an interface except that it may have attributes and participate in generalizations with other classes.

Figure 30 shows an example of an abstract operation. The implementation for such an operation must be provided by a subclass.

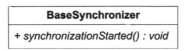

Figure 30. An abstract operation

Properties and constraints on operations

As the syntax for operations shows, you can associate a property with each operation. The following properties are valid:

isQuery
> Indicates that an operation will return a value without modifying the class in any way. This property can be mapped to a const method in C++.

sequential
> Indicates that an operation must be called in only one thread of execution at a time. In other words, the operation is not thread safe, and the caller must control access properly. The behavior of a sequential operation is considered undefined if multiple threads use it at a single time.

guarded
> Similar to sequential, but the operation itself enforces the rule that only a single thread can call the method at any

given time. Concurrent calls to this operation are handled sequentially by the operation, without any effort on the caller's part. This property can be mapped to a synchronized method in Java.

concurrent
Indicates that an operation is guaranteed to be thread safe and can handle multiple concurrent callers.

UML defines three constraints that you may use on your operations:

precondition
Expresses what the state of the system must be before the associated operation can be invoked.

postcondition
Expresses what the state of the system will be after the operation completes.

bodyCondition
Expresses constraints on the return value. The bodyCondition may be overridden by subclasses, so it is separate from the postcondition.

Because constraints can be lengthy (they are often restrictions on attributes specified using OCL), you can place them in a note and attach the note to an operation with a dashed line. Figure 31 shows an example of a bodyConstraint.

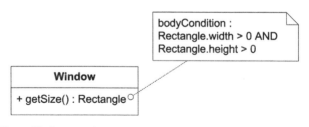

Figure 31. A constraint on an operation

Operation scope

Operations are typically scoped to an instance of a class, in which case, they are considered to be of *instance scope*. However, operations can be shared between objects (static), in which case, they are considered to be of *classifier scope* and are underlined, as shown in Figure 32.

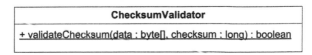

Figure 32. An operation of classifier scope

Template classes

Several programming languages allow a developer to design a class without specifying the exact types on which the class operates. At a later time, the user of a template class can specify the target types and retain type safety during compiles. UML allows modeling of template classes by simply overlaying a dotted box that contains the template parameters in the upper-right corner of a regular class, as shown in Figure 33.

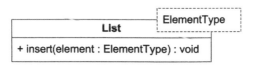

Figure 33. A template class

Associating a real type with a template class is called *binding*. UML provides two ways of representing template binding. The first, *implicit binding*, is similar to the C++ syntax for templates, in which you simply define a class named with the template arguments, as shown in Figure 34.

Figure 34. Implicit binding

The alternative to implicit binding is *explicit binding*, which is represented using a stereotyped relationship, as shown in Figure 35.

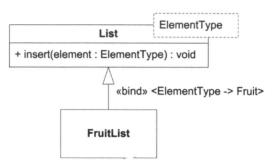

Figure 35. Explicit binding

Interfaces

An *interface* is another type of UML classifier used to define services that a class or component must provide. Interfaces are named according to the same rules that apply to naming classes, but they contain only operations, not attributes. Interface names commonly begin with a capital I—for example, IATAPIDevice.

In their expanded form, interfaces are drawn as stereotyped classes (see "Stereotypes," earlier in the text) with an empty or omitted attribute compartment.

The distinction between operations and methods is particularly important with interfaces because they may not include methods (operation implementations). Figure 36 shows the graphical representation of an interface in expanded form.

«interface»
ReservationValidator
+ validateRoute(routeInfo : Route) : boolean

Figure 36. An expanded interface

Interfaces can also be represented in a more compact form as a simple circle. There is no specification difference between the two representations; they are used merely to distinguish interfaces from classes visually. The circle (or *icon*) representation is often used when showing interface realization (see the earlier section, "Class relationships") in the stick-and-lollipop form. Figure 37 shows the icon representation of the interface shown earlier in Figure 36.

ReservationValidator

Figure 37. The icon version of an interface

It is common to use an interface to define the services provided by a subsystem. In this case, a package (see the next section, "Package Diagrams") stereotyped as subsystem is shown realizing an interface. Some UML models actually make use of both class and subsystem realization of an interface, depending on the level of detail that the particular class diagram is showing. Subsystem implementers may need to see exactly which classes realize the service defined by the interface, whereas clients of the service may only care which component or subsystem contains the requisite classes.

Strictly speaking, UML allows any visibility for operations defined for an interface, but language mappings may require that interface methods be public.

Package Diagrams

Packages are all-purpose containers used to group related UML elements, including other packages. Packages are named according to the same convention used to name classes. Packages have a different graphical representation than classes; their names are located in the center of a folder, as shown in Figure 38.

Figure 38. A sample package

Packages are typically used in class and component diagrams, but they can be used to group just about anything.

Packages represent distinct namespaces within a model, so package-owned model elements must have unique names within the package. However, those same names can be used for different elements in another package. UML also treats different types of elements (e.g., classes and components) as though they are in different namespaces, meaning that a class may have the same name as a component, regardless of whether they belong to the same package. It is important to note that giving the same name to two UML elements is highly discouraged. Elements can be owned by only one package, but packages can access or import other packages.

Visibility of Package Elements

Packages introduce another level of visibility for contained elements. Each element within a package can be given one of the following levels of visibility:

public
> Indicates that the element can be used by anyone outside the package.

protected
> Indicates that the element can be used only by packages that inherit from the package.

private
> Indicates that the element can be used only by other elements contained within the same package.

Nested packages are considered to be within the same package and therefore can access *public*, *protected*, and *private* elements of their parent package. Note that this is different from Java's notion of packages.

Contents of a package, along with their visibility, can be displayed using the same folder icon. When showing the detailed contents of a package, the name of the package is moved to the folder tab and the package contents are displayed within the folder. The contents can be represented by simple text, by rectangles containing element names, or, in rare cases, by using a graphical representation similar to the composition arrow. Figure 39 shows a textual representation of package contents.

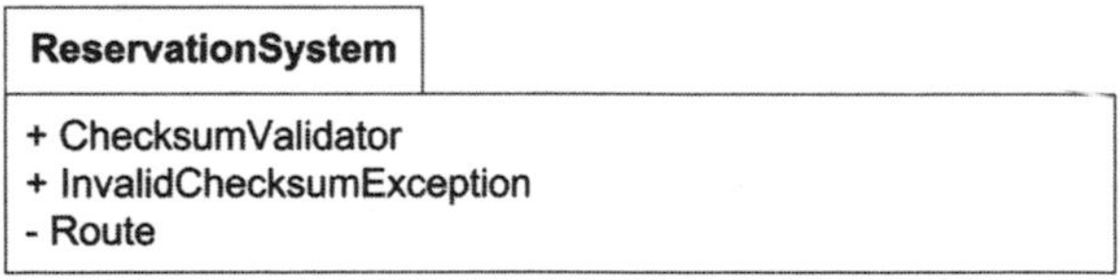

```
┌─────────────────────────┐
│ ReservationSystem        │
├──────────────────────────────────┐
│ + ChecksumValidator              │
│ + InvalidChecksumException        │
│ - Route                          │
└──────────────────────────────────┘
```

Figure 39. A package showing textual content and visibility

Figure 40 shows rectangular notation for package contents. Figure 41 shows package contents using the UML anchor symbol.

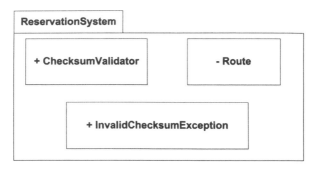

Figure 40. A package showing rectangular content notation

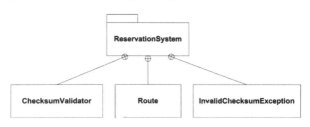

Figure 41. Package represented using composition-style notation

Visibility is shown using the standard +, #, and - symbols, for *public*, *protected*, and *private*, respectively. As with operations, some tools introduce the symbol ~ to show Java's default (*package-protected*) visibility.

Dependencies Between Packages

Packages almost always rely on other packages when used in a real system. Packages can relate to each other by depending on other packages or inheriting their elements. UML defines two stereotypes to refine package dependencies further:

Access

Shows that a package uses the public elements of another package but that each element must be fully qualified using the longer, colon-separated path name.

Import
> Shows that a package actually incorporates another package's public elements into its own namespace. This introduces possible naming conflicts, but it does not require elements to be scoped.

Typically, access and import are represented similarly in language mappings. Figure 42 shows sample package dependencies. ReservationSystem imports DBUtilities and uses elements in the AirlineNetworking package.

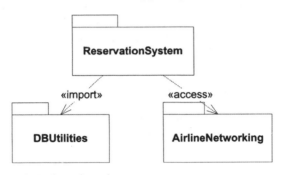

Figure 42. Package dependencies using stereotypes

Package Stereotypes

There are five predefined UML stereotypes that are specific to packages:

Facade
> Indicates that though a package is incomplete, it is a specific representation of another, larger package. The relationship between a facade package and the larger package is similar to the relationship between an interface and a class implementing that interface along with others.

Framework
Indicates that a package contains classes and interfaces that provide application-level patterns. These classes and interfaces are often used to implement subsystems within a larger application.

Stub
Indicates that a package does not contain the full implementation of a set of functionality, but rather the package contains only the minimum requirements necessary to define the service. Typically, a stub package contains interfaces, abstract classes, or proxy classes. Stub packages are deployed frequently on the client side of CORBA or EJB services.

Subsystem
Indicates that a package holds a self-contained set of functionality. A full system is often made up of several subsystems and subsystems are typically comprised of multiple components. Subsystems may depend on other subsystems but offer considerable functionality on their own.

System
Indicates that a package contains an entire system. This stereotype is typically used for a top-level package containing several nested packages, further dividing the system into subsystems and components.

Figure 43 shows a package stereotyped as a subsystem.

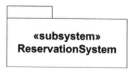

Figure 43. A stereotyped package

Package Tagged Values

Packages support UML-tagged values. There are no pre-defined UML tags for packages; however, it is common to use tags for things such as author names, descriptions, versions, and external version requirements (e.g., *application major version 2.x*). Figure 44 shows a package with a version tag.

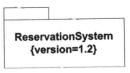

Figure 44. A package with tagged values

Merging Packages

UML 2.0 introduces the concept of merging packages. A fairly complex set of rules governs package merging, but the basic concept is similar to the set that governs package imports. However, with merged packages, classes with the same name in the source and target packages establish a generalization relationship. For more information about package merging, see *UML 2.0 in a Nutshell* (O'Reilly) or the UML specification.

Composite Structures

When you model a system, you often repeat complex relationships such as design patterns or models of real-world elements. UML 2.0 introduces a new concept called *composite structures* to capture these patterns. You indicate composite structures using notation similar to class diagrams, but you can specify the intent of your pattern.

Structures

Structures are interconnected elements set up at runtime to implement some piece of functionality. Each structure is made up of one or more objects and connectors. A *connector* is a communication link between the instances of the classes at either end. Each connector has an optional name and class type. The connector is represented as a solid line between the elements with the name of the connector written near the line. The syntax for naming a connector is:

    name : classname

where:

name

> Is the name of the connector used by collaborations to reference the structure

and:

classname

> Identifies some class that represents the connection between the two endpoints

The communication between the elements of the structure is not specified by UML; it could be as simple as a method call or as complex as a web service. Figure 45 is an example of a structure.

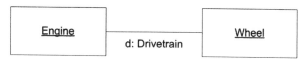

Figure 45. Composite Structure for an engine

You can add constraints to a connector using a note. For example, you can state that the drivetrain must be all-wheel drive, as shown in Figure 46.

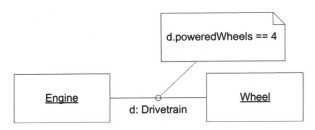

Figure 46. Constraint on a connector

Finally, you can specify multiplicity for each end of the connector by placing a number near the element. You can use an integer number, a range, or an asterisk (*) to indicate unlimited multiplicity. Figure 47 shows a structure representing four wheels connected to an engine.

Figure 47. Multiplicity on a composite structure

Ports

The point of composite structures is to build higher-level functionality. A port indicates that a structure offers some functionality without detailing how that functionality is realized internally. It is represented as a small square associated with another UML element, typically a component. If you draw the port inside the element, it is a protected port, available only to the composite structure itself. If you draw it on the edge of the element, it is a public port and is available to external users. The name of the port is written near the square. Figure 48 shows a public port.

Figure 48. Public port on a component

Provided and required interfaces

You can indicate that a port offers or needs a particular interface by using the ball-and-socket notation for interfaces (see "Interfaces," earlier in the text). If you need to use multiple interfaces, simply put them in a comma-separated list. Figure 49 shows an example of a structure with provided and required interfaces.

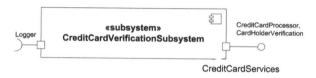

Figure 49. Ports with provided and required interfaces

Realizing ports

Ports represent a piece of functionality that must be implemented at some point. You indicate this relationship by drawing a connector from the port to the classifier that realizes the functionality. If the element with the port realizes the functionality itself, you show a state inside of the classifier. This type of port is called a *behavioral port*. Figure 50 shows a behavioral port being realized by the owning class.

If a port's functionality is realized by other elements, which is common in the case of subsystems or components, you simply show a connector to the realizing element. Figure 51 shows a port on a component realized by a class.

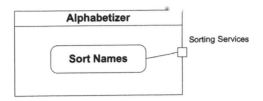

Figure 50. A behavioral port

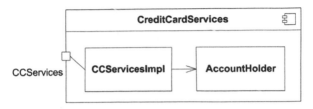

Figure 51. A port linked to an internal implementation

You can have multiple connectors coming from a single port and leading to different internal elements, but UML does not specify how data is processed. Be sure to document what multiple connector means in your model (forwarded to all receivers, round-robin, etc.).

Typing ports

In general, a port represents some classifier that simply passes the information that it receives to the classifier that realizes its functionality. However, UML 2.0 allows you to explicitly type a port as a different classifier, enabling you to manipulate the data passing through the port. For example, if you have an HTTP port on a web server component, you can explicitly type the HTTP port as a DenialOfServiceFilter and intercept data before your component processes it. Note that any classifier used for a typed port must realize any interfaces that the port offers. You write the name of the classifier, followed by the type, near the port. Figure 52 shows an example of a web server component.

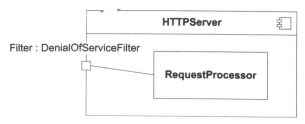

Figure 52. A port explicitly typed as a DenialOfServiceFilter

Structured Classes and Properties

Structured classes with properties allow you to model complex structures and provide a context for their use. For example, before UML 2.0, you could show that four wheels were owned by a car but not that they had to be owned by the *same* car. To indicate a structured class, you draw the normal classifier rectangle with the class name in the first compartment. Draw the classes that make up the structure in the second compartment.

Figure 53 depicts a sample structured class representing a car, engine, and wheels. This diagram shows that a car has one engine and four wheels. More importantly, it shows that an engine and the associated wheels are linked to a single car.

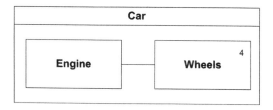

Figure 53. Car with engine and wheels

Structured classes can also indicate whether they exclusively own an inner element or whether it is shared with other classes. If the structured class exclusively owns an inner element (composition), draw the inner element with a solid rectangle. If the element is shared with other classes (aggregation), draw the rectangle with dashed lines.

You can show how elements are instantiated within a structured class by first underlining the inner element's name to indicate that you're showing an instance of the element. Then, specify values for each of the element's attributes by placing an equals sign and the desired value after the attribute type. Figure 54 shows a car with a specific brand of tires.

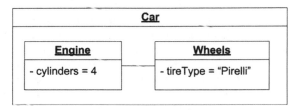

Figure 54. Specifying instance information in a structured class

Collaborations

Composite structures are commonly used to model patterns, called *collaborations* in UML 2.0. You define a basic collaboration as a dashed oval with the name of the collaboration inside. For example, Figure 55 shows a collaboration named Observer/Observable after the design pattern of the same name.

Figure 55. A simple collaboration

To show the details of the collaboration, simply place the classifiers involved inside a second compartment in the collaboration oval. Figure 56 shows details for an Observer/Observable collaboration.

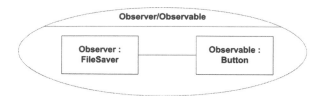

Figure 56. Details of the Observer/Observable collaboration

Putting the elements outside of the oval and drawing connectors from it to each classifier is another way to show the details of a collaboration. Place the role name near the connector line. The advantage of this notation is that you can show more details of each classifier; the disadvantage is that you can't show the connectors between the elements. Figure 57 shows the Observer/Observable collaboration with the classifiers outside of the oval.

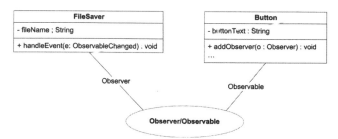

Figure 57. Observer/Observable collaboration with details outside

Collaboration occurrences

Once you've defined a collaboration, you can show it being used with a *collaboration occurrence*. You depict a collaboration occurrence with the same dashed oval but also use dashed lines to the classes playing the appropriate roles in your collaboration. For example, Figure 58 shows an Observer/Observable collaboration being used by a Button and a ButtonListener.

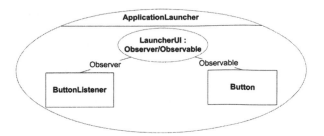

Figure 58. A collaboration occurrence of the Observer/Observable collaboration

Component Diagrams

Component diagrams are similar to class diagrams but concentrate on higher, subsystem-level abstractions. Component diagrams typically contain components, interfaces, and their relationships.

Components

A *component* is a physical piece of a system, such as a compiled object file, piece of source code, shared library, or Enterprise JavaBean (EJB). Figure 59 shows the default representation for a component. As with classes, the name of a component can be fully qualified using :: to separate package names.

Figure 59. A simple component

UML allows users to replace the default representation of a UML element when using stereotypes. For example, rather than use the icon shown in Figure 59, modeling tools typically use a dog-eared piece of paper to represent a component stereotyped as a document. Customized representations of UML elements are frequently used in component diagrams because UML provides standard stereotypes, though not icons, for the following types of components:

document

    The stereotyped component represents some type of textual document (Word, text, RTF, etc.).

entity

    The stereotyped component represents a business concept.

executable

    The stereotyped component represents a complete executable that can be run on a node.

file

    The stereotyped component represents some type of file, such as source code, system data, input, or output.

library

    The stereotyped component represents a shared or static library of compiled code.

process

    The stereotyped component can fulfill functional requests (contrast with entity).

realization

    The stereotyped component doesn't have its own specification; it is a realization of a separate specification component.

service

    The stereotyped component is a stateless component that can fulfill service requests.

specification
> The stereotyped component provides and requires interfaces but doesn't actually realize them. It is typically associated with a realization component.

subsystem
> The stereotyped component is a relatively large component and makes up a piece of a larger system. It usually indicates a self-contained functionality.

table
> The stereotyped component represents a database table.

To further expose information, components can have multiple compartments, such as interfaces realized by the component or classes contained in an EJB archive. Figure 60 shows a component with a compartment displaying contained classes.

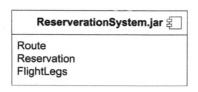

Figure 60. A component showing contained classes within a compartment

Alternatively, contained classes can be represented using dependencies, as shown in Figure 61.

Components can have operations listed on them, but the operations are typically available only through the interfaces that they realize. UML allows components to have attributes, but you won't see this often. Information, such as manifest values in a Java *.jar* file, is more appropriately modeled as tagged values, as shown in Figure 62.

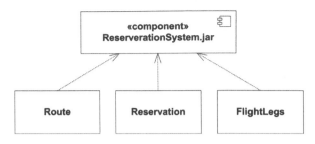

Figure 61. An alternate view of contained classes, using dependencies

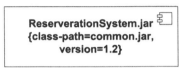

Figure 62. A component showing manifest values in a .jar file

Component Modeling

As with class diagrams, component diagrams are used to show the static assembly of a system. Component diagrams can illustrate how subsystems relate and which interfaces are implemented by which components. Associations, generalizations, dependencies, and realizations can be used in component diagrams, as shown in Figure 63.

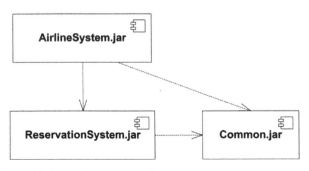

Figure 63. A sample component diagram

Usually, a component diagram shows one or more interfaces and their relationships to other components. Interfaces are central to component-based development and modeling, so they are typically the focus of component diagrams. A component-interface relationship can be represented with the graphic stick-and-lollipop representation, as shown in Figure 64.

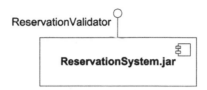

Figure 64. Interface realization using stick-and-lollipop notation

Interface realization can also be represented using the standard realization arrow used in class diagrams, as shown in Figure 65.

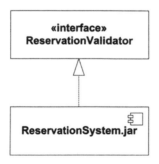

Figure 65. Interface realization using the realization arrow

More often, components and interfaces are included in the same diagram to illustrate interface realization and the dependencies of other components on those interfaces. Technically, component-to-component dependency is a component-to-interface dependency, as well as a realization to the component implementing the interface. Dependency is represented with the same arrow used for class dependency or by a socket to the interface ball, as shown in Figure 66.

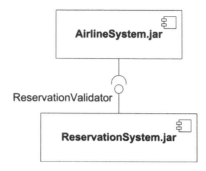

Figure 66. Interface realization and component dependencies

Component Views

There are two basic views of components in a system: white-box and black-box. The *white-box view* shows the internal details of a component and the classifiers that comprise it. Figure 67 shows a white-box view of an event distribution system.

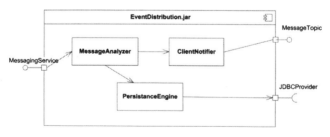

Figure 67. White-box view of a component

The *black-box view* of a component shows provided and required interfaces and any other details needed to convey the guaranteed behavior of the component; it does not offer any details of how that functionality is realized. Figure 68 shows a black-box view of the same event distribution system.

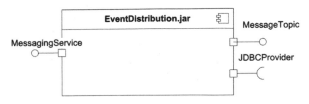

Figure 68. Black-box view of a component

Deployment Diagrams

Deployment diagrams show the physical nodes on which a system executes, and they usually contain artifacts, nodes, components, and the associations between the nodes and components.

Artifacts

Artifacts model physical pieces of information in your system. For example, a user's manual, training material, or password file can all be modeled as artifacts. One of the most common uses for artifacts is to model compiled versions of components. For example, a Java-based message passing framework could be compiled into a Java *jar*. You could model that final *jar* using an artifact.

An artifact is represented by the normal classifier rectangle with a dog-eared piece of paper in the upper-right corner. Figure 69 shows a sample artifact.

MessagePassingFramework.jar

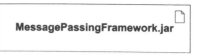

Figure 69. A sample artifact

As with other UML classifiers, artifacts can have properties, which you indicate on an artifact as you would on any other classifier—by putting them in their own compartment and using the attribute notation for classes. Figure 70 shows an example of properties on an artifact.

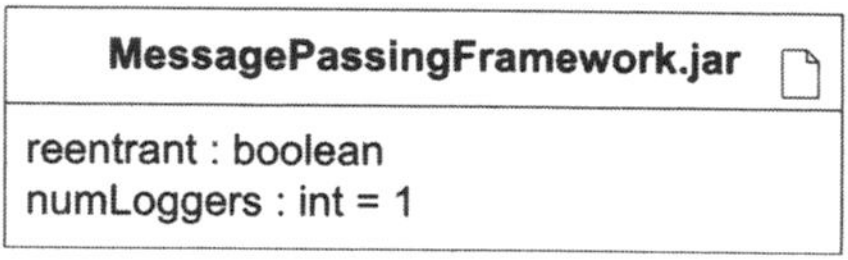
MessagePassingFramework.jar
reentrant : boolean
numLoggers : int = 1

Figure 70. An artifact with attributes

Like other UML classifiers, artifacts represent *types* of things. To show an instance of an artifact—for example, a copy of your jar installed on `Webserver1`—simply underline the artifact's name, as shown in Figure 71.

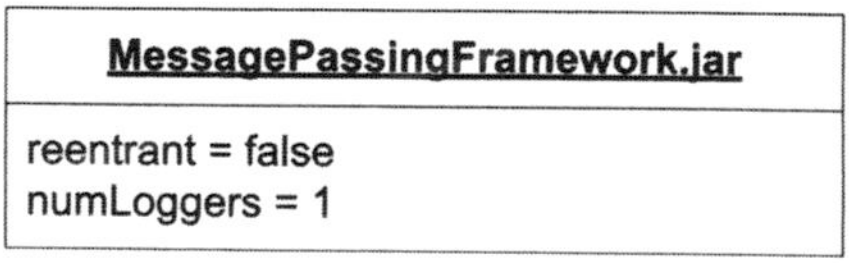
MessagePassingFramework.jar
reentrant = false
numLoggers = 1

Figure 71. An instance of an artifact

Note that because people rarely use artifacts to represent types, UML does allow for non-underlined artifacts to be interpreted as instances, as long as it doesn't cause any confusion in the model.

An artifact often represents a *manifestation* of some other UML classifier. To indicate a manifestation, draw a dependency arrow with the «manifest» stereotype from the artifact to the component it represents. Figure 72 shows how the MessagePassingFramework.jar artifact is a manifestation of the MessagePassingFramework component.

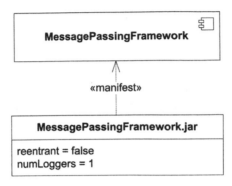

Figure 72. The manifestation of a component as an artifact

Nodes

A *node* is a physical entity that executes one or more components, subsystems, or executables (although, strictly speaking, subsystems and executables are simply stereotyped components). A node is rendered as a cube and, as with all other UML classifiers, has a unique name within its package. Figure 73 shows a simple node.

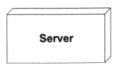

Figure 73. A node

Nodes can have multiple named compartments that show extra information, such as deployed components, as shown in Figure 74. Attributes and operations can be specified for nodes.

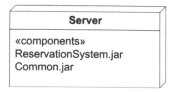

Figure 74. A node with multiple compartments

Rather than list the contents of a node in a compartment, you can represent deployed components using dependency relationships between the node and the components, as shown in Figure 75.

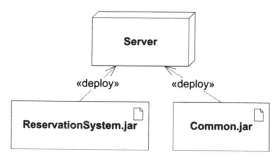

Figure 75. A node with its deployed components

Node Modeling

Relationships between nodes are represented as associations, and they can be stereotyped to capture additional information. Though UML allows for all association types (e.g., composition, aggregation, and simple associations) to be used for nodes, the simple association line is usually used.

Associations between nodes are called *connections*. Figure 76 shows three nodes and their connections.

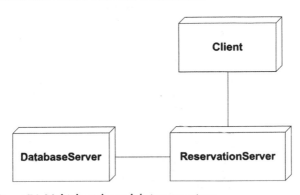

Figure 76. Multiple nodes and their connections

As with classes and components, nodes can be organized within packages. Usually, nodes are stereotyped and rendered using custom icons when modeling anything but the simplest system. Common node stereotypes include database, server, client, and backup server, though UML does not provide any standard stereotypes for nodes. Figure 77 shows a typical deployment diagram using stereotyped nodes.

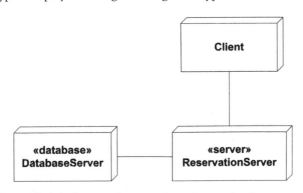

Figure 77. A deployment diagram using stereotyped nodes

Specialized Nodes

There are two types of specialized nodes that are particularly useful to modelers: *execution environments* and *devices*. Execution environments model pieces of software that provide some set of services or guaranteed environmental capabilities to hosted artifacts. The classic example of an execution environment is a J2EE application server. UML doesn't define any execution environments itself, but it expects end users to create profiles that will define stereotypes to capture particular environments.

To indicate that a node is an execution environment, simply stereotype it with the environment name. Figure 78 shows a node stereotyped as a J2EE Application Server.

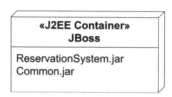

Figure 78. Execution environment with two deployed artifacts

The second type of specialized node, the device node, represents a physical hardware component involved in a system. You indicate a device node using the stereotype «device». Because you can embed deployment nodes in UML, you can show an execution environment running on a particular device. Figure 79 shows our J2EE Application Server running on a BLADE Server.

Deployment Specifications

Most modern deployment environments offer some way to tell the hosting environment how a particular component should be configured and what it needs. A *deployment*

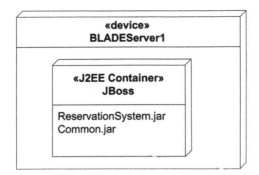

Figure 79. A device node with an execution environment

specification is a set of properties, often represented as attributes on a classifier, that provides any information that a particular artifact may need at runtime or to configure its host.

UML allows you to capture this information with a stereotype called «deployment spec». To show that a deployment specification is related to particular artifact, draw a dashed line with an open arrow from the deployment specification classifier to the artifact. For example, Figure 80 shows deployment information for a web application.

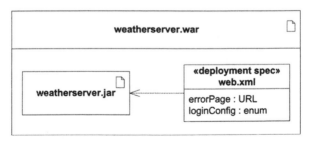

Figure 80. An artifact and its deployment specification

Behavioral Diagrams

Behavioral diagrams are used to capture the dynamic execution of a system, including required functionality, state transitions within classes, components, entire subsystems, and object interactions. Behavioral diagrams can illustrate the flow of execution in a system, including simple object interactions, component migration, or complex multithreaded system flows.

Behavioral modeling encompasses the following diagrams:

- Use case diagrams
- Interaction diagrams
- Collaboration diagrams
- Statechart diagrams
- Activity diagrams

The various behavioral diagrams are closely related. For example, sequence diagrams can be created from collaboration diagrams and vice versa. Behavioral diagrams are also closely linked with static diagrams. Class diagrams show realizations of the requirements captured in use case diagrams, and sequence diagrams show the interactions of objects depicted in object diagrams.

Use Case Diagrams

Use case diagrams capture the requirements of a system. The term *use case* often refers to a document that describes a particular piece of functionality that a system must provide. Strictly speaking, however, a use case is a UML element, whereas the document describing a use case is a *use case document*. Throughout this section, the term *use case* refers to the UML notion of a use case and not to the document.

Use Cases

Typically, use cases are short phrases or sentences that sum up a distinct piece of functionality that a system offers a user. As with other UML elements, use cases are often grouped into packages and can be referenced using their fully qualified name. Along with the name of a use case, a sequence of events describes the system's behavior when the use case is invoked. There is no UML-defined notation for recording this sequence of events, so it is often described in a separate use case document, which is simply a text document created using any word-processing program. A use case is represented in a use case diagram by an ellipse, as shown in Figure 81.

Figure 81. A use case

Use cases are at a higher level of abstraction than other UML elements and describe, from the user's perspective, functionality that a system must provide. Use cases do not specify how the system actually implements the functionality, rather they are intended to communicate desired functionality from end users to project managers and actual developers.

Actors

Use cases are associated with one or more actors. An *actor* is a role that a user takes when invoking a use case. A single user can be represented by multiple actors because a user can fulfill multiple roles. Likewise, a single actor can represent multiple users. An actor is represented as a stick figure with its name written underneath, as shown in Figure 82.

System Administrator

Figure 82. An actor

Actors do not always need to represent human users; they can be used to represent external systems with which a modeled system interacts. For example, you might model a robotic-tape subsystem as an actor. Actors help draw the boundary between what needs to be implemented as part of the system being modeled and what exists outside of the system.

Use cases and actors are connected using associations. When using associations on use case diagrams, the directionality of the association indicates only who initiates the interaction, not the direction of information flow. For example, Figure 83 shows both human and machine systems interacting with a use case from an ATM system. Obviously, there is interaction with the customer while the withdrawal takes place; however, the ATM never initiates a withdrawal by contacting the user.

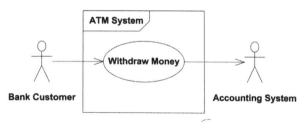

Figure 83. Human and machine actors and use cases

A bidirectional association indicates functionality that can be invoked by either the system or the actor.

By definition, anything modeled with a use case is considered inside your system. Anything that is external to your system—other systems, identity checking procedures, etc.—should not be modeled as a system use case. To help make this clear in use case diagrams, use cases are listed inside a rectangle, whereas external systems are shown outside of it. The rectangle is called a *system boundary* and it represents where your system ends and the rest of the world begins. See Figure 83 for an example of a system boundary.

Use Case Modeling

Use cases often relate to other use cases within the same system by employing generalization, extension, or inclusion.

Use case generalization

Use case generalization behaves in exactly the same way that class generalization does; a specialized use case inherits the behavior of the original use case. Then, the specialized use case can replace or enhance the behavior, but it adheres to the external contracts of the original use case. Generalization is modeled using the same generalization arrow used with classes, as shown in Figure 84.

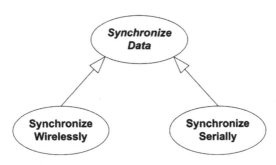

Figure 84. Use case generalization

Use case inclusion

A use case can include the behavior of another use case. The included use case is not used by itself; it can be used only as part of a larger, separate use case. Most often, use case inclusion is used when pulling out common functionality shared between use cases. When including another use case, the containing use case states explicitly in its flow of events when the included use case is invoked. For example, an online purchasing system may include a use case to authenticate customers within a larger use case for purchasing an item. In this example, customer authentication would never happen outside of the context of the larger goal.

Use case inclusion is shown using a dependency arrow that is stereotyped with include, as shown in Figure 85.

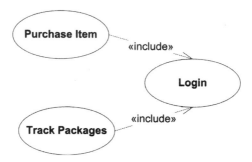

Figure 85. Use case inclusion

Use case extension

Use case extension encapsulates a distinct flow of events that are not considered part of the normal or basic flow. They are not necessarily exceptional conditions, but they are large enough parts of functionality to detract from the focus of the base use case into which they're incorporated.

When using a use case extension, the author of the base use case document states explicitly the points at which the base use case can be extended by other use cases. Unlike included use cases, extension use cases can be complete, standalone use cases that simply plug into a larger system at these author-defined extension points. For example, the previously mentioned online-purchasing system cannot log all communication involved in placing an order unless it is in some sort of debugging mode. The Purchase Item use case can be extended by a separate Log Debugging Info use case if the debugging criteria are met.

Use case extension is modeled using a dependency arrow stereotyped with extend and named with the extension point's name, as shown in Figure 86.

Figure 86. Use case extension

Use Case Realization

Because use cases capture requirements at a functional level, UML provides a mechanism for tracing functional requirements to their actual implementation, called *use case realization*. As with interface realization, use case realization is represented using the realization arrow between a collaboration and a use case. A collaboration looks similar to a use case ellipse drawn with a dashed line, and it is typically linked to one or more UML diagrams. Figure 87 shows an example of a collaboration in a use case realization.

Usually, a single collaboration draws in elements from multiple packages and contains its own diagrams that show how these elements interact to provide the required functionality.

Figure 87. A use case realization

Collaborations use both static and behavioral diagrams to show how a use case is implemented. Diagrams within a collaboration often stop at subsystem or interface boundaries, in which case, the details of subsystem functionality are left to subsystem modeling.

Collaborations can relate to other collaborations in that one may provide more detail in a particular area than another, so one collaboration may be dependent on another. To model collaboration relationships, use a dependency arrow stereotyped as refine. Figure 88 shows that the Order Distribution collaboration refines the Order Processing collaboration.

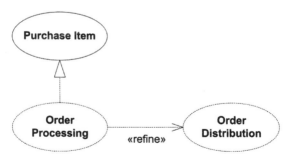

Figure 88. Collaboration refinement

Use Case Documents

While technically not part of UML, use case documents are closely related to UML use cases. A use case document is a text document that captures the detailed functionality of a use case. Such documents typically contain the following parts:

Brief description

Used to describe the overall intent of the use case. Typically, the brief description is only a few paragraphs, but it can be longer or shorter as needed. It describes what is considered the *happy path*—the functionality that occurs when the use case executes without errors. If needed, it can also include critical variations on the happy path.

Preconditions

Conditionals that must be true before the use case can begin to execute. Note that this means the author of the use case document does not need to check these conditions during the basic flow, as they must be true for the basic flow to begin.

Basic flow

Used to capture the normal flow of execution through the use case. The basic flow is often represented as a numbered list that describes the interaction between an actor and the system. Decision points in the basic flow branch off to alternate flows. Use case extension points and inclusions are typically documented in the basic flow.

Alternate flows

Used to capture variations to the basic flows, such as user decisions or error conditions. There are typically multiple alternate flows in a single use case. Some alternate flows rejoin the basic flow at a specified point, whereas others terminate the use case.

Postconditions

> Conditionals that must be true for the use case to complete. Postconditions are usually used by testers to verify that the realization of the use case is implemented correctly.

Interaction Diagrams

Interaction diagrams are a whole class of diagrams in UML 2.0 focusing on communication between elements. UML 2.0 has the following interaction diagrams:

Sequence diagrams

> By far the most common, sequence diagrams show a time-based view of messages between elements.

Communication diagrams

> A close relative of sequence diagrams, communication diagrams place more emphasis on which elements are talking to which and less emphasis on the time-based nature of the communication.

Interaction overview diagrams

> Interaction overview diagrams represent interactions using a simplified version of the activity diagram notation.

Timing diagrams

> Timing diagrams focus on specific timings between when messages are sent and received. They are useful for modeling real-time systems and anything with time-sensitive messaging.

Sequence Diagrams

Sequence diagrams emphasize the time-based flow of events. A sequence diagram shows the participating objects along the top of the diagram, with messages listed from top to bottom in order of execution. The basic sequence diagram has a frame around the outside. In the upper left corner of that

---

frame is a box with a "dog-eared" corner containing sd followed by the name of the diagram. Figure 89 shows a simple sequence diagram.

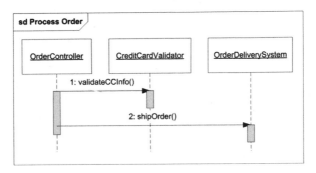

Figure 89. A simple sequence diagram

Interaction participants

Participants in a sequence diagram are indicated by rectangles along the top with the following notation:

    object_name [selector] : class_name ref decomposition

where:

object_name
Specifies the name of the instance involved in the interaction

selector
Is an optional part of the syntax that can be used to choose a particular instance from a collection of instances, such as an array or list

class_name
Specifies the name of the type of the participant

Decomposition
Is an optional part of the name referencing another interaction diagram that shows further details about how this participant handles the messages it receives

You can use the keyword self to indicate that the participant is the classifier that owns the sequence diagram.

Object creation and deletion

Each object has a dashed lifeline running vertically down the diagram that shows when the object comes into existence and when it is destroyed. Objects created during the time covered by a sequence diagram are often shown directly above the message that creates them. Object creation is represented by a dashed line with an open arrow head extending from the creating object's lifeline to the newly created object's lifeline. You should use the «create» stereotype to indicate that the message causes the target object to be instantiated. Figure 90 shows object creation in sequence-diagram form.

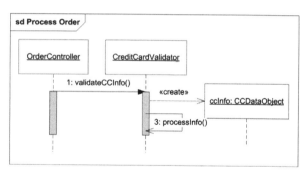

Figure 90. A sequence diagram showing object creation

Likewise, objects destroyed during the time covered by a sequence usually are not drawn beyond the message that causes the destruction. A destruction message is represented by a solid line with a filled arrow pointing to the target object's lifeline and stereotyped with «destroy». The lifeline of the object is terminated with an X, as shown in Figure 91.

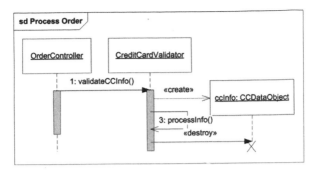

Figure 91. A sequence diagram showing object destruction

Object messages

Each message passed to an object invokes some type of response, called an *action*. The most basic type of message is a call message. Call indicates that the message is an invocation of an operation on the target object. An object can call an operation on itself, in which case, the operation is modeled as a link back to the object. A message that results in an operation invocation is named for the invoked operation. UML allows you to specify arguments to the operation as part of the message name; however, most UML tools do not support this.

The syntax for a message is:

```
attribute = signal_or_operation_name
  ( arguments ) : return_value
```

where:

attribute
  Is an optional part of the syntax that provides a named holder (variable) for the return value from the call. You can then reference this attribute in later messages.

signal_or_operation_name
  Specifies the name of the signal to send or the operation to invoke.

arguments
> Indicates a comma-separated list of arguments to pass to the operation or signal.

return_value
> Explicitly shows what the return value is.

Synchronous calls (meaning the caller is blocked until the target operation is complete) are represented with a filled arrow, as shown in Figure 92.

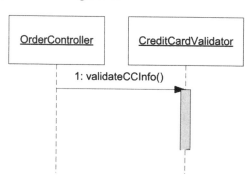

Figure 92. A sample call message

Show asynchronous calls (meaning the caller doesn't wait for the return value) with an open arrow, as shown in Figure 93.

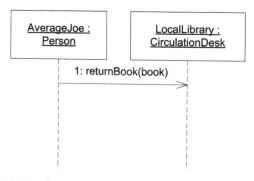

Figure 93. Sample asynchronous call

Return is a special type of message that indicates the result of a previous call to an operation. Return is represented as a dashed line ending in an arrow that points to the object receiving the return value. The link is often named for the returned object. Figure 94 shows a return value from a call.

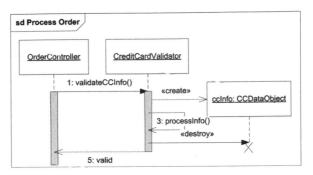

Figure 94. A sequence diagram showing return values

Return values can arrive out of order because asynchronous messages do not require the caller to wait for the result. To show that a return value may arrive after other messages are sent, simply draw the return arrow such that it intersects the original caller further down its lifeline than other messages. For example, you could send in three orders for takeout food before the first one is ready to be picked up, as shown in Figure 95.

Lost and found messages

UML 2.0 introduced the concept of messages that do not reach their destination (*lost* messages) or are from unknown sources (*found* messages). Note that lost and found are relative terms; the receiver or sender might only be unknown with respect to your current sequence diagram. Lost messages are commonly used to show how a system handles a network failure resulting in an undelivered message. Found messages are commonly used for modeling exception

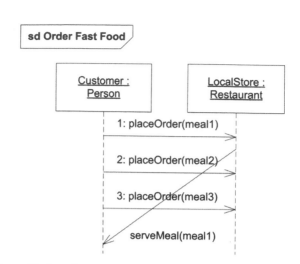

Figure 95. Asynchronous messages with an out of order response

handling—you don't necessarily care who threw the exception; you simply want to show how it is handled.

To indicate a lost message, simply draw a filled dot at the end of a message arrow, as shown in Figure 96.

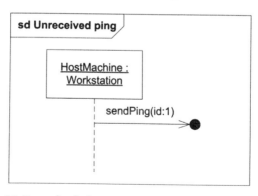

Figure 96. Example of a lost message

Conversely, a found message originates from a filled dot, as shown in Figure 97.

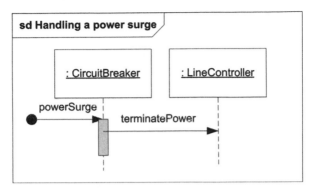

Figure 97. Example of a found message

State invariants

You can place invariant conditions across lifelines in a sequence diagram to indicate that the condition must be true for all following messages to execute. This should be considered similar to an assertion in Java or C++; it should not be used to model a conditional evaluation. See the next section, "Interaction operators," for a better way to model conditional execution.

You indicate a state invariant by placing a Boolean expression between curly braces across object lifelines. The expression must evaluate to true for any messages below the expression to be evaluated. Figure 98 shows a sample state invariant.

Interaction operators

UML 2.0 greatly improves the ability of a sequence diagram to capture conditional and looping logic. The basic building block is a *combined fragment*. A combined fragment is a frame around a set of messages with an interaction operator

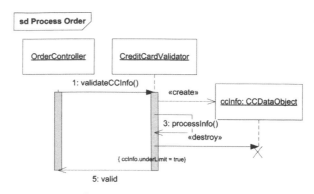

Figure 98. Example state invariant

written in the upper-left corner. Figure 99 shows a simple *critical* combined fragment (see later in this section for a definition of critical).

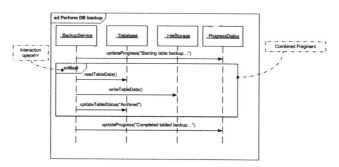

Figure 99. Sample combined fragment

The following are the common interaction operators available in UML 2.0:

alt

> An *alternative* is an if-then-else execution. To indicate the alternative flows, simply divide the combined fragment with a dashed line. Each flow can have a Boolean

guard condition, written between square brackets, that must evaluate to true for the flow to execute. You may use the reserved else guard condition to indicate a flow that should execute if none of the others evaluate to true. Figure 100 shows a simple example of alternatives.

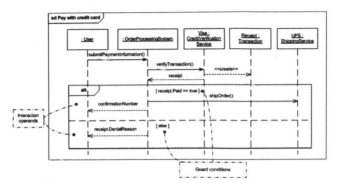

Figure 100. Example alternative operator

opt

An *option* is a combined fragment that executes only if its guard condition evaluates to true. Conceptually, options are similar to alternatives with only one flow.

break

A *break* is a combined fragment with a guard condition stipulating that if the condition evaluates to true and the fragment executes, then the enclosing interaction should terminate.

par

A *parallel* fragment indicates that the messages in the different regions can be interleaved and executed in parallel. Note that the relative ordering within a region must be maintained. See Figure 101 for an example of a parallel section.

neg

A *negative* fragment indicates a set of messages that are invalid in the current context. For example, you could indicate that you cannot call Show( ) on a window after Dispose( ) has been called.

critical

A *critical* region is a set of messages that must be treated as an atomic block, meaning they cannot be interrupted by another thread or process. critical is often used to model semaphores. See Figure 101 for an example of a critical section.

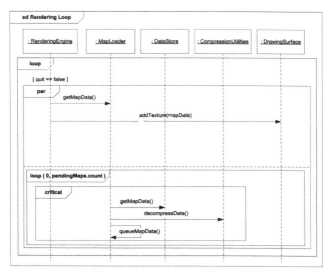

Figure 101. Example loop and parallel operators

assert

An *assertion* is a fragment that is the only valid execution path. Assertions are typically associated with a state invariant to guarantee the state of a system. If the state invariant evaluates to false, the fragment will not execute (which is illegal because it's an assertion).

loop

A *loop* allows you to model messages that should be repeated a number of times. After the loop operator, you should express the minimum and maximum number of times that the messages should repeat with the following syntax:

```
loop ( min, max )
```

where min and max are optional. To show unbounded, simply use an asterisk (*). An example of a loop is shown in Figure 101.

Communication Diagrams

Communication diagrams focus on the communication between elements rather than the sequencing of the messages passed. A communication diagram can represent behavior within a component, a use case, or even across systems.

Communication diagrams use the same building blocks that sequence diagrams use: objects and links over which messages are sent. However, communication diagrams label each link with information indicating the direction and type of message sent between elements. Technically, abstract classes and interfaces cannot be instantiated directly; still, it is not uncommon to see both used on communication diagrams. Interfaces or abstract classes on communication diagrams represent instantiations of a realizing or concrete class. Interfaces and abstract classes can be used to represent an arbitrary implementation because they carry contracts for behavior with them.

A link in a communication diagram usually includes a sequence number showing the order in which the message occurs, the name of the operation being invoked, and an arrow indicating the direction in which the message flows. Figure 102 shows typical links in a communication diagram.

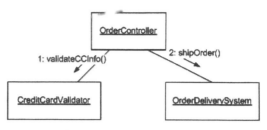

Figure 102. A simple communication diagram

Most UML tools can convert from one to the other because communication diagrams and sequence diagrams are so closely related.

Interaction Overview Diagrams

Interaction overview diagrams represent interactions using a cross between an activity diagram and a sequence diagram. They are designed to help illustrate the overall flow of execution through a modeled system. An interaction overview diagram begins with a filled dot and transitions to one or more combined fragments showing relevant sequences.

Table 2 shows how to model a sequence diagram concept in an interaction overview diagram.

Table 2. Mapping sequence diagram concepts to interaction overview diagrams

Sequence diagram concept	Interaction overview notation
Combined fragments	Decision and merge nodes
Parallel interactions	Fork and join nodes
Loops	Cycles in the diagram transitions
Lifelines of participants	Use the keyword lifelines in the diagram title, followed by a comma-separated list of each participant's name and type.

Figure 103 is an example of an interaction overview diagram.

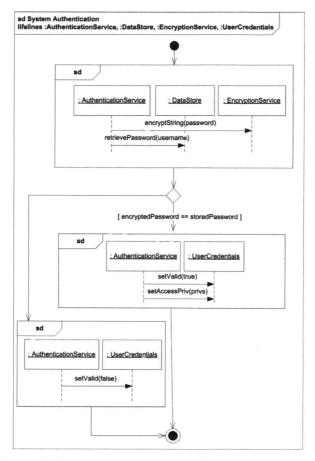

Figure 103. A sample interaction overview diagram

Timing Diagrams

Timing diagrams are a special version of interaction diagrams that focus on the specific timings of messages. They are ideal for showing specific times that messages must be sent or received, or for showing how an element changes its internal state over time.

Timing diagrams are read left to right, with states of a lifeline running vertically along the left side. Label time ticks along the bottom of the diagram with your desired unit of time. Draw a line from right to left showing the transition through the various states as time passes. For each state transition, you can write in the name of the message that triggered the transition. For example, Figure 104 is a timing diagram showing a greatly simplified mail server progressing through three states: Idle, Authenticated, and Transmitting.

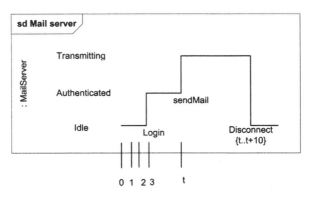

Figure 104. Timing diagram with transitions and time constraints

Statechart Diagrams

Statechart diagrams show the various stages (or *states*) of an entity during its lifetime. A statechart diagram can be used to show the state transitions of methods, objects, components, subsystems, or entire systems. The UML specification describes two types of state machines: behavioral and protocol. *Behavioral state machines* show the behavior of a particular element in your system. *Protocol state machines* show the behavior of a protocol and they are not tied to a particular implementation. For example, you could model the mail protocol SMTP using a protocol state machine without discussing whether you are modeling Microsoft Exchange or Postfix.

States

A *state* represents a condition of a modeled entity for which some action is performed, some stimulus is received, or some condition is met elsewhere in a system. Typically, an entity remains in a state for a measurable amount of time; however, UML supports modeling of instantaneous states to help model a flow of operation.

Each state is rendered as a rectangle with rounded corners. The name of a state can be represented as a tab attached to the top of the state; however, this is usually reserved for composite states (see the upcoming section, "Composite States"). As with classes, state names are usually rendered in a name compartment, as shown in Figure 105.

Waiting for Connection

Figure 105. A state

Actions and Activities

States can have a second compartment containing actions or activities performed while an entity is in a given state. An *action* is an atomic execution and therefore completes without interruption. An *activity* is a more complex collection of behavior that may run for a long duration. An activity may be interrupted by events, in which case, it does not run to completion. Each action or activity can have an *action label* defining an event that triggers the action or activity. UML predefines four action labels:

entry
> The specified action triggers upon entering the state.

exit
> The specified action triggers upon exiting the state.

do
> The specified action triggers after an entry action and runs until completion or an externally triggered state transition. Note that completion of the action may trigger an event that causes the entity to leave the state.

include
> The specified action refers to another statechart (a submachine) that contains other internal states (or substates).

The syntax for an action label and action is as follows:

```
action-label-or-event (parameters)
[guard-condition]/action-expression
```

This syntax contains the following user-defined elements:

action-label-or-event
> An action or event that triggers the action described in action-expression.

parameters
> Objects or values made available to the action. Commonly, parameters are attributes of the event triggering the action, or the enclosing object represented by the state machine.

guard-condition
> A Boolean expression indicating some additional criteria that must be met before the action specified by action-expression can occur. Note that the square brackets are part of the syntax and must be present if you are using a guard condition.

---

action-expression

> A representation of the behavior that occurs as a result of the trigger event. The behavior can be described in natural language, pseudocode, or real code expressions.

Figure 106 shows a state with multiple actions.

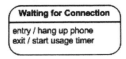

Figure 106. A state with multiple actions

Transitions

The initial state of a state machine is represented as a solid black circle, connected by a transition to the first state of an entity. Transitions between states are represented as directed arcs between states. As with states, transitions can have triggers, guard conditions, and actions. A transition can be labeled with the event or action that creates the entity.

To indicate details controlling a transition, you use the same notation that you use with states:

> *trigger* [*guard*] / *effect*

where:

trigger

> Specifies which condition caused this transition to occur. Typically, it's an event received by the state machine.

guard

> Specifies a constraint evaluated by the state machine before the transition is permitted to occur. If the guard condition evaluates to false, the transition is not considered.

effect

> Specifies an activity that executes when the transition occurs.

Figure 107 is an example of a state machine having transitions with triggers and effects.

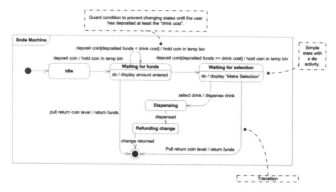

Figure 107. A state machine with several transitions

The final state of a state machine, represented as a circle around a filled dot, indicates the completion of a state machine and can trigger a completion event in an enclosing composite state.

Signals

Signals are used if the transition from one state to another may cause other information to be sent or received by your system. You can show a signal being sent during a transition by drawing an unlabeled transition from the source state to a rectangle with a triangular point on its right side, followed by another unlabeled transition to the destination state. Write the name of the signal inside the rectangle. Figure 108 shows a signal being sent during a state transition.

If the reception of a signal is critical to your state transition, you can use a rectangle with an inverted triangle. Draw an unlabeled transition from the source state to the rectangle and another unlabeled transition to the destination state. Place the name of the received signal in the rectangle.

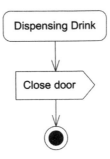

Figure 108. A transition that sends a signal

Figure 109 shows a signal being received before transitioning to the next state.

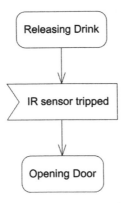

Figure 109. Example of a signal being received during a transition

Composite States

A composite state is comprised of other substates and is depicted with states and state transitions contained inside. Technically, a statechart diagram is a composite state that represents a state machine of a modeled entity. However, the outermost composite state is not usually shown. Figure 110 shows a simple composite state.

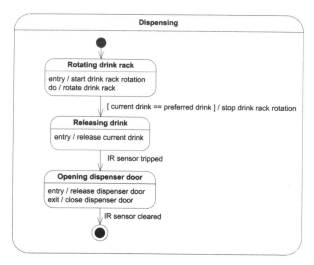

Figure 110. A simple composite state

If you do not want to show the detail of a composite state on your diagram, you can hide any inner states and use the composite state icon at the bottom right. Figure 111 shows a collapsed composite state.

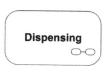

Figure 111. Hidden composite state

Regions

A composite state can be subdivided into multiple concurrent state machines, known as *regions*. Regions are separated by a dashed line. Each one should have its own initial and final pseudostates (see the later section, "Pseudostates," for a fuller definition). A transition to the composite state corresponds to a transition to the initial state of each region; they execute in parallel. The composite state remains active and is not considered complete until all regions have reached their final states. Regions are frequently used to model concurrent threads within a larger system. Figure 112 shows an example of a composite state with regions.

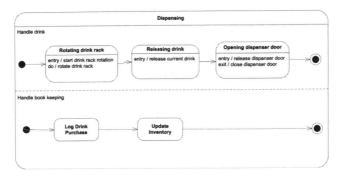

Figure 112. A composite state with two regions

Submachine states

A *submachine state* is a specialized version of a composite state. It defines a set of internal state transitions using a separate state machine and then references that state machine when needed. For example, you could develop a state machine showing an authentication procedure for your system, then reference that machine from a Logging On state in a different diagram. To use a submachine state, simply place a colon (:) after your state name, followed by the state machine that you are referencing. Figure 113 shows a simple logon procedure and Figure 114 shows a submachine state referencing it.

Figure 113. A state machine capturing a trivial logon procedure

**Logon :
LognProcedureSM**

Figure 114. A submachine state referencing the logon procedure state machine

Concurrent Transitions

To support concurrent states, UML allows for concurrent transitions. *Concurrent transitions* represent either forking or joining when transitioning between states. They are represented by a thick, solid line with one or more transition lines leading to the next state or states. Figure 115 shows concurrent transitions, demonstrating both forking and joining.

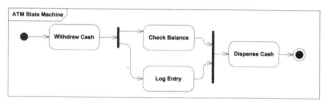

Figure 115. Concurrent transitions

In Figure 115, the transition out of the Withdraw Cash state makes both Check Balance and Log Entry concurrent. Then, both Log Entry and Check Balance must complete before the machine can transition to Dispense Cash.

Protocol State Machines

Protocol state machines capture the behavior of protocols rather than a particular system element. For example, you could model TCP/IP handshaking or penguin courting rituals using protocol state machines.

States in protocol state machines represent stable conditions in which the system is in a known condition and is not processing information. There are several rules associated with protocol state machines:

- entry, exit, and do activities cannot be used.
- States can have invariant conditions. Place invariants in square brackets below the name of the state.
- Place the keyword protocol in curly braces after the state machine name.
- Transitions in protocol state machines have preconditions, triggers, and a postcondition. The precondition must be true before a state machine can change states and the postcondition must be true after the transition. Express preconditions and postconditions with the following syntax:

    `[precondition] event / postcondition`
- Each transition is associated with no more than one operation on the owning classifier.
- Protocol state transitions cannot have any effect activities because they do not model a particular classifier's behavior.

Figure 116 is a dramatically simplified SMTP protocol state machine.

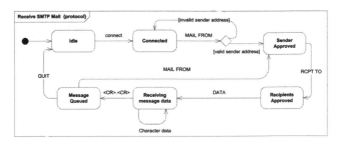

Figure 116. Simplified SMTP protocol state machine

Pseudostates

UML defines several pseudostates that represent specific behavior or conditions within a state machine. Table 3 shows the common pseudostates and their meanings.

Table 3. State machine pseudostates

Pseudostate name	Symbol	Description
Initial pseudostate	●	The starting point of a state machine.
Choice	◇	Execution of the state machine will choose between different transitions based on guard conditions.
Deep history	(H*)	Used inside a state region, a transition to this pseudostate indicates that the state machine should resume with the last substate in the given region.
Entry point	○	A possible target for a transition into a composite state. Must be labeled by writing its name near the state.
Exit point	⊗	A possible source for a transition from a composite state. Must be labeled by writing its name near the state.
Fork and join	├→	Represents a split in the execution of a state machine into parallel execution paths. A join represents the reuniting of those paths and waits until all paths have hit the pseudostate before continuing.
Junction	●	Brings several possible transitions together into a single pseudostate. One or more transitions may then leave the pseudostate.
Shallow history	(H)	Used inside a region to show that a transition to this pseudostate should resume with the last substate at its level.
Terminate node	✕	Causes the state machine to terminate.

Activity Diagrams

As with state diagrams, *activity diagrams* are used to capture behavioral flow information; however, they concentrate on transitions between states without showing external stimuli. State transitions within an activity diagram occur simply because of the completion of actions associated with previous states.

Activity diagrams capture state transitions for a given entity, such as a class, operation, use case, or subsystem, and are frequently used to model algorithms or procedures. As with state diagrams, activity diagrams have an initial state shown as a filled circle and a final state shown as a filled circle within a ring.

Action States

An activity diagram is made up of multiple action states. An *action state* represents a state with an entry action and an implicit transition to the next state, although it can have a guard condition that restricts this transition. An action state is represented as a rectangle with rounded sides. The action associated with the state is simply written in the rectangle, either as a short phrase or as pseudocode. When using pseudocode, you can reference attributes or links of the owning entity. Figure 117 shows an example of an action state.

> Submit Requisition

Figure 117. An action state

Activity Edges

A transition between action states is called an *activity edge*, which is represented as a straight line ending with an arrow that points to the next state. Activity edges cannot have events associated with them, but they can have guard conditions. Figure 118 shows several action states and the activity edges between them.

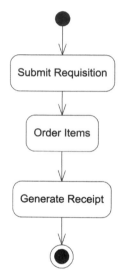

Figure 118. Transitions between action states

Object flows

UML 2.0 defines a special type of activity edge called an object flow. An *object flow* allows you to select data according to a specified criteria before it heads into a given state. To show data flowing into an action, you can use an *object node*, which is simply a rectangle containing the name of some type of data for which it acts as a source. You can then link the object node with an action that processes the given data using an object flow. Figure 119 shows a simple object node that produces students.

Figure 119. An object node that produces students

You can apply a selection behavior to an object flow to choose which objects are allowed to flow into the action node. To indicate a selection, attach a note to the object flow, stereotype it with «selection», and write your selection criteria in it. (It is typically written using pseudocode or OCL, but can be natural language if necessary.) Figure 120 illustrates filtering the data heading into the action.

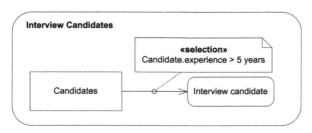

Figure 120. Selecting objects heading into an action

You can indicate that an action requires a specific type of data using a pin. A *pin* is a small rectangle on the edge of an action that is labeled with the type of data required. For example, we could indicate that the Alphabetize Roster action requires Students by placing a pin on the action, as shown in Figure 121.

You can use *output pins* to represent data produced by an action. The notation is the same; it's simply a question of whether an activity edge enters the action or leaves it.

Figure 121. Using a pin to indicate the type of data needed by an action

Figure 122 shows a Register Students action that produces students for the Alphabetize Roster action.

Figure 122. Examples of input and output pins

As with selections, you can apply transformations to map one type of data into another as it passes through an object flow. Note that the UML specification clearly states that transformations *may not* have side effects on the data. To indicate a transformation, attach a note to the object flow, stereotype it with «transformation», and write the pseudocode or OCL required to convert the data in the note. Figure 123 shows extracting GPA information from Students to compute the class average.

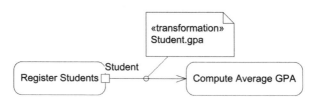

Figure 123. Example of using a transformation to extract data from a Student object

Exceptions

You indicate that an action can throw an exception by using an *exception pin*, which is represented by a rectangle with a small triangle near it. Figure 124 shows that the Register

Students action could throw an exception, causing the activity diagram to transition to the Schedule Followup action. Note that the Schedule Followup action requires a Student Registration Form piece of data in its input pin.

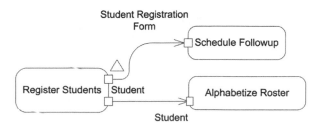

Figure 124. Using an exception pin

You can show that an exception is handled by a particular action with an *exception handler node*. In the typical case, the action is abandoned if an exception occurs in a normal action. However, if an action has an exception handler, flow transitions to the exception handler when the exception occurs. Output from the exception handler is then available to the node that would have executed next (if the exception hadn't occurred). You indicate an exception handler by using a lightning bolt activity edge from the protected action to the handler, with the exception's name next to the lightning bolt. Figure 125 shows an exception handler.

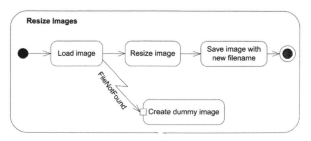

Figure 125. Example of an exception handler for the Load Image action

Connectors

To simplify large diagrams, you can use connectors to break up your flow. Each connector is simply a circle with a label written inside, often just a single letter. Show an activity edge to the connector; later, you can use the same connector with an activity edge heading to the next action. The connector has no functional meaning and is simply a notation for making large diagrams more readable. Figure 126 shows a simple connector labeled with the letter *c*; this diagram is equivalent to Figure 118.

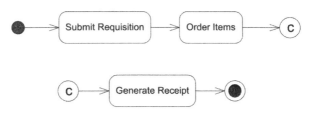

Figure 126. A connector breaking up an activity diagram

Subactivity State

A subactivity state is used to embed a separate activity diagram within a larger diagram. Upon entering a subactivity state, the initial action state of the subactivity diagram is entered. After the final action state of the subactivity diagram completes, execution resumes with the state following the subactivity state.

A subactivity state is rendered like an action state, but with an icon representing an activity diagram in the lower right, as shown in Figure 127. Details of the subactivity state would appear on a separate activity diagram.

Figure 127. A subactivity state

Decision and Merge

A single transition from a state can split into multiple transitions, depending on guard conditions. You can also indicate a conditional in a note stereotyped with «decisionInput» and attached to the decision point. Decision points in an activity diagram are represented by diamonds; a single transition enters each diamond and multiple transitions come out. UML predefines one guard condition, else, which can be used if all the guard conditions can be false. Figure 128 shows a decision that results in different action states.

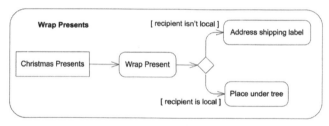

Figure 128. A decision in an activity diagram

After a decision, the various paths through an activity diagram can join into a single path with a merge. A merge also appears as a diamond, but it has multiple transitions leading into the diamond and only one leading out. The transition leading out of the diamond cannot have a guard condition. Figure 129 shows several action states merging into one action state.

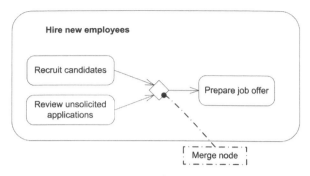

Figure 129. A merge in an activity diagram

Fork and Join Nodes

A *fork node* splits the current flow into multiple concurrent flows. It is typically used to model threading in a software system. A fork node is represented by a vertical bar with one activity edge heading into it and multiple ones heading out. You can illustrate a flow terminating using a *flow final node*, which is drawn as a circle with an X in it. When a flow reaches a flow final node it stops, but other flows may continue executing within the action. Figure 130 shows parallelizing the process of hiring a new employee using a fork node.

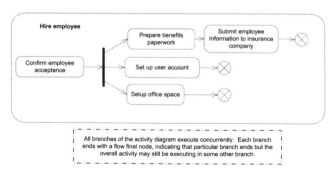

Figure 130. An example fork node in an activity diagram

A *join node* is effectively the opposite of a fork node; it has multiple input edges with a single output edge. Execution stops at the join node until all incoming flows have reached it, at which point, it transitions out of the single exit activity edge. A join node uses the same vertical bar as a fork node. Figure 131 shows merging separate dinner activities before serving a meal.

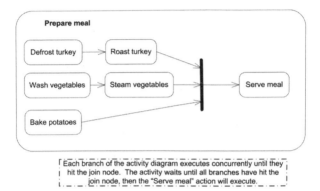

Figure 131. An example join node in an activity diagram

Partitions

An activity diagram can be divided into multiple vertical or horizontal sections called *partitions*. You can place a label at the top (or left) of each partition that indicates how the activities in the partition are related. Partitions do not have to indicate which object or component carries out a given action; they are useful to capture how activities fit together in a higher, business-level workflow. Each partition is separated from the others by solid vertical or horizontal lines. Edges can cross partitions freely. Figure 132 shows an activity diagram divided into partitions.

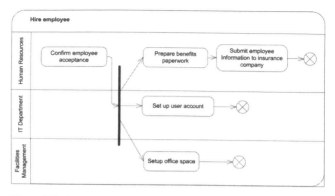

Figure 132. Partitions in an activity diagram

Signals

Sending and receiving signals are common occurrences in an activity diagram. UML provides two symbols to use with signals. The first, a rectangle with a concave triangle on one side of it containing the signal name, indicates receipt of a signal. Signal reception is represented as part of an activity diagram by showing a transition from a previous state to the signal symbol, followed by a transition to the next state. You can show the object that sent the signal on the activity diagram with a dependency on the signal reception symbol.

The second signal symbol, a rectangle with a convex triangle at one end, indicates transmission of a signal. Its placement in an activity diagram is the same as it is with signal reception. You can represent the receiver by showing a dependency from the signal symbol to the object receiving the signal.

See Figures 108 and 109, earlier in the text, for examples of signals being sent and received during a transition.

The Object Constraint Language (OCL)

The Object Constraint Language 2.0 is an addition to the UML 2.0 specification that allows you to write constraints in well-defined grammar that—in theory—can be validated by a UML modeling tool. This section gives a brief overview of the most frequently used parts of the OCL.

OCL can be used almost anywhere in UML but is usually associated with a classifier using a note. OCL has several built-in types that can be used in your expressions:

Boolean
> Must be either true or false and supports the logical operators and, or, xor, not, implies, and if-then-else.

Integer
> Can be any integer value and supports the operators *, +, -, /, and abs( ) for absolute value.

Real
> Can be any decimal value and supports the operators *, +, -, /, and floor( ).

String
> Indicates a series of letters, numbers, or symbols. Supports the operators concat( ) (for concatenation), size( ), and substring( ).

Basic Syntax

Every OCL expression has a sense of *context*, meaning it knows which classifier it applies to. You express this classifier in OCL using the keyword self. For example, if you wanted to enforce the rule that the number of students in an object of type Course is always greater than 10, you could write:

```
self.numStudents > 10
```

You can follow associations between classes by simply refer-ring to the association end names as though they were attributes. So, if our fictitious Course had an association named Instructor, we could check the instructor's salary with the expression:

```
self.Instructor.salary < 1000000.00
```

If an association isn't named, you could use the name of the class at the end of the association instead. So, if Instructor was of type Faculty, we could rewrite the previous expres-sion as:

```
self.Faculty.salary < 1000000.00
```

If an association can be null, you could determine if the value is set by using the OCL operator notEmpty( ). For example, we could use the following syntax to make sure our Course has an instructor:

```
self.Instructor->notEmpty( )
```

You can insert comments into an OCL expression by prefix-ing them with two dashes (--). For example:

```
-- Must always have an instructor for a course
self.Instructor->notEmpty( )
```

You can state explicitly the context of your expression by using the OCL keyword context followed by the class name that you want to reference. So, we could be explicit about our Course class with the following expression:

```
context Course
self.Instructor->notEmpty( )
```

You can also alias the context by placing a name followed by a colon (:) before the type name. For example, we could alias our Course to c with the following expression:

```
context c : Course
c.Instructor->notEmpty( )
```

Constraints on Operations

In addition to constraints on classes, you can place constraints directly on operations. The notation is similar except that you specify a fully qualified operation name instead of using the context as a class name. You can also indicate whether your constraint is a precondition or postcondition by using the keywords pre and post, respectively. For example, we can confirm that a Student has taken prerequisites before registering for a Course with the following constraint:

```
context Course::registerStudent(s : Student) : boolean
pre: s.hasPrereqs = true
```

When writing a postcondition, use the keyword result to refer to the value returned from the operation. For example, the following constraint ensures that a student has completed prerequisites before registering for a class and that the operation registerStudent returned true:

```
context Course::registerStudent(s : Student) : boolean
pre: s.hasPrereqs = true
post: result = true
```

When writing postconditions, you can use the @pre keyword to refer to a value of some element *before* the operation runs. This is useful when verifying that counters are updated or lists are empty, etc. For example, the following constraint ensures that there is one more student in the Course after registration:

```
context Course::registerStudent(s : Student) : boolean
pre: s.hasPrereqs = true
post: result = true AND self.numAttendees = self.
numAttendees@pre + 1
```

Finally, you can express the results of a query operation using the keyword body, which is useful for indicating what a query operation will return. For example, we can show that getAttendees() will return the Students associated with a Course with the following expression:

```
context Course::getAttendees() : List
body: self.students
```

Constraints on Attributes

As with operations, you can place constraints on attributes by specifying the fully qualified attribute name and type. You can use the keyword init to specify an initial value for the attribute. For example, the following expression states that the initial number of seats available in a Course is 30:

```
context Course::numSeats : int
init: 30
```

You can use the derive keyword to specify the value of an attribute after its initial value. For example, the following expression shows that the number of seats in a Course is equal to 30 minus the number of registered students:

```
context Course::numSeats : int
derive: 30 - self.numAttendees
```

Conditionals

OCL supports basic conditional logic to evaluate constraints. Note that you cannot influence execution flow of the system; you can only influence what constraint is applied to your target. For example, the following expression indicates that if a Student's GPA is below 2.0, he does not have a year of graduation:

```
context Student
if self.GPA < 2.0 then
  self.yearOfGraduation = 0000
else
  self.yearOfGraduation = 2006
endif
```

OCL uses the keyword implies as shorthand for conditional clauses. If the first half of an expression evaluates to true, then the part of the expression following the implies keyword must also evaluate to true or the expression is invalid. If the first half evaluates to false, the whole expression is considered true. For example, we could enforce that students with a GPA below 2.0 do not have a year of graduation with the following shortened expression:

```
context Student
self.GPA < 2.0 IMPLIES self.yearOfGraduation = 0000
```

Note that we are not checking the value of the student's GPA if it is above 2.0, though you could do that with another implies expression.

You can declare variables in expressions using the let and in keywords. Variables are useful for cleaning up your constraints; you do not need to repeat long expressions in conditions. For example, we could declare a variable to hold the year of graduation with the following expression:

```
context Student
let yog : int = self.yearOfGraduation in
self.GPA < 2.0 IMPLIES yog = 0000
```

You can define a variable to use across multiple constraints using the keyword def instead of let. The syntax is the same as shown in the previous expression using let:

```
context Student
def yog : int = self.yearOfGraduation
self.GPA < 2.0 IMPLIES yog = 0000
```

However, now you can use yog in multiple constraints.

Collections

OCL supports several different kinds of collections. For the most part, you can treat the various collection types as a generic Collection (OCL's base class). Collection offers the following operations:

select(*Boolean expression*)
>   Pulls elements that meet the given expression out of a collection. For example, you can select students with high GPAs from our Course with the following expression:
>
>   ```
>   self.students->select(GPA > 3.5)
>   ```

exists(*Boolean expression*)

> Returns true if there is at least one element in the collection that meets the given condition. For example, we could determine whether there is at least one student passing our Course with the following expression:

```
self.students->exists(GPA > 2.0)
```

forAll(*Boolean expression*)

> Returns true if all of the elements in the collection meet the given expression. For example, we could determine whether all of the students in a Course have paid their tuition with the following expression:

```
self.students->forAll(tuitionPaid = true)
```

notEmpty( )

> Evaluates to true if there is at least one element in the collection. For example, we could determine whether our Course contains at least one student with the following expression:

```
self.students->notEmpty( )
```

reject(*Boolean expression*)

> Removes elements from a collection that meet the given expression (inverse of select). For example, we could evaluate our collection of high GPA students and remove ones with disciplinary action against them using the following expression:

```
self.students->select(GPA > 3.5)->
reject(disciplinaryAction = true)
```

Index

We'd like to hear your suggestions for improving our indexes. Send email to
index@oreilly.com.

Related Titles from O'Reilly

Software Development

Applied Software Project Management

Designing Interfaces

Essential Business Process Modeling

Enterprise Service Bus

Head First Design Patterns

Head First Design Patterns Poster

Practical Development Environments

Prefactoring

The Art of Project Management

UML 2.0 in a Nutshell

UML 2.0 Pocket Reference

O'REILLY®